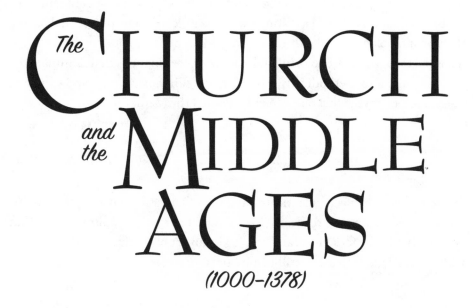

The CHURCH
and MIDDLE
the
AGES
(1000–1378)

"Catholics have endured for too long the distorted and prejudiced caricatures of Medieval culture, which have for five centuries provided fuel for anti-Catholic and anti-Christian polemics. Medieval Christianity is a glorious and multifaceted phenomenon, and one of which Catholics should be proud. Steve Weidenkopf's book on the High Middle Ages does a fine job of helping to dispel the misconceptions about this era and assisting Catholics in reclaiming an essential part of their own theological and cultural heritage. This book provides up-close introductions to many of the colorful and attractive personalities that dominate the period, while also methodically, carefully, and fairly examining and exposing the numerous myths that obscure our vision of the Medieval age."

Jamie Blosser
Professor of theology at Benedictine College
Author of *Positively Medieval*

"Steve Weidenkopf packs an amazing amount of narrative and analysis into this accessible book, helping readers see the Church not only as culture-maker but also as troubled by foes inside and out, led by an array of saints and sinners, and with a fragile glory that can still inspire us if we understand it aright."

David M. Wagner
Author of *The Church and the Modern Era*

"Knowing history is a crucial part of Catholic apologetics and this book is a superb place to start. Weidenkopf debunks myths and dispenses illusions about one of the most misrepresented and misunderstood periods of history. If you've never read history, accompany Weidenkopf as he dives deep in this engaging and comprehensive presentation."

Derya Little
Author of *From Islam to Christ*

"Steve Weidenkopf's book is an excellent and engaging primer on the persons, events, and culture of the High Middle Ages. Catholics should take a lively interest in Weidenkopf's work, as it affirms the intrinsic connection between the Catholic faith and the hallmarks of Western civilization that developed in the medieval period. I recommend it highly."

Phillip Campbell
Historian and author of *Heroes and Heretics of the Reformation*

≡ RECLAIMING CATHOLIC HISTORY ≡

The CHURCH and the MIDDLE AGES

(1000-1378)

Cathedrals, Crusades, and the Papacy in Exile

STEVE WEIDENKOPF

Series Editor, Mike Aquilina

AVE MARIA PRESS AVE Notre Dame, Indiana

≡ RECLAIMING CATHOLIC HISTORY ≡

The history of the Catholic Church is often clouded by myth, misinformation, and missing pieces. Today there is a renewed interest in recovering the true history of the Church, correcting the record in the wake of centuries of half-truths and noble lies. Books in the Reclaiming Catholic History series, edited by Mike Aquilina and written by leading authors and historians, bring Church history to life, debunking the myths one era at a time.

The Early Church
The Church and the Roman Empire
The Church and the Dark Ages
The Church and the Middle Ages
The Church and the Reformation
The Church and the Age of Enlightenment
The Church and the Modern Era

Series introduction © 2019 by Mike Aquilina

Founded in 1865, Ave Maria Press is a ministry of the United States Province of Holy Cross.

www.avemariapress.com

Paperback: ISBN-13 978-1-59471-953-0

E-book: ISBN-13 978-1-59471-954-7

Cover images © Getty Images.

Cover and text design by Andy Wagoner.

Printed and bound in the United States of America.

Library of Congress Cataloging-in-Publication Data
Names: Weidenkopf, Steve, author. | Aquilina, Mike, editor.
Title: The church and the Middle Ages (1000-1378) : cathedrals, crusades,
    and the papacy in exile / Steve Weidenkopf, Mike Aquilina.
Description: Notre Dame, Indiana : Ave Maria Press, 2020. | Series:
    Reclaiming Catholic history ; book 3 | Includes bibliographical
    references. | Summary: "Steve Weidenkopf shines a spotlight on some of
    the Catholic Church's greatest saints and dispels nine misconceptions.
    He explores the shifting centers of power, reform movements, and
    tensions both within the Church and between Church and State while also
    examining the challenges the Church faced in the eleventh through
    fourteenth centuries"-- Provided by publisher.
Identifiers: LCCN 2020029508 | ISBN 9781594719530 (paperback) | ISBN
    9781594719547 (ebook)
Subjects: LCSH: Church history--Middle Ages, 600-1500. |
    Papacy--History--To 1500. | Church and state--History--To 1500.
Classification: LCC BX1068 .W45 2020 | DDC 270.4--dc23
LC record available at https://lccn.loc.gov/2020029508

TO DR. KRIS BURNS (1950–2019)

For your service, dedication, and love of the Church and Christendom College, and for your support, encouragement, and friendship to me.

Requiescat in pace

While recognizing that what is Catholic is not necessarily medieval, and what is medieval is not necessarily Catholic, we must at the same time admit that there has never been an age in which European culture was more penetrated by the Catholic tradition, or in which Catholic ideals found a fuller expression in almost every field of human activity. The age of St. Bernard and St. Francis, of St. Thomas and St. Bonaventure, of St. Louis and Dante, is perhaps the one age in which all that was strongest and most living in European thought and society accepted Catholic principles and consecrated itself to the service of God and the Church.[1]

—*Christopher Dawson (1889–1970)*

Contents

⊨ RECLAIMING CATHOLIC HISTORY ⊨
Series Introduction

"History is bunk," said the inventor Henry Ford. And he's not the only cynic to venture judgment. As long as people have been fighting wars and writing books, critics have been there to grumble because "history is what's written by the winners."

Since history has so often been corrupted by political motives, historians in recent centuries have labored to "purify" history and make it a bare science. From now on, they declared, history should record only facts, without any personal interpretation, without moralizing, without favoring any perspective at all.

It sounds like a good idea. We all want to know the facts. The problem is that it's just not possible. We cannot record history the way we tabulate results of a laboratory experiment. Why not? Because we cannot possibly record all the factors that influence a single person's actions—his genetic makeup, the personalities of his parents, the circumstances of his upbringing, the climate in his native land, the state of the economy, the anxieties of his neighbors, the popular superstitions of his time, his chronic indigestion, the weather on a particular day, the secret longings of his heart.

For any action taken in history, there is simply too much material to record, and there is so much more we do not know and can never know. Even if we were to collect data scrupulously and voluminously, we would still need to assign it relative importance. After all, was the climate more important than his genetic makeup?

But once you begin to select certain facts and leave others out—and once you begin to emphasize some details over others—you have begun to impose your own perspective, your interpretation, and your idea of the story.

Still, there is no other way to practice history honestly. When we read, or teach, or write history, we are discerning a story line. We are saying that certain events are directly related to other events. We say that events proceed in a particular manner until they reach a particular end, and that they resolve themselves in a particular way.

Every historian has to find the principle that makes sense of those events. Some choose economics, saying that all human decisions are based on the poverty or prosperity of nations and neighborhoods, the comfort or needs of a given person or population. Other historians see history as a succession of wars and diplomatic maneuvers. But if you see history this way, you are not practicing a pure science. You are using an interpretive key that you've chosen from many possibilities, but which is no less arbitrary than the one chosen in olden days, when the victors wrote the history. If you choose wars or economics, you are admitting a certain belief: that what matters most is power, wealth, and pleasure in this world. In doing so, you must assign a lesser role, for example, to the arts, to family life, and to religion.

But if there is a God—and most people believe there is—then God's view of things should not be merely incidental or personal. God's outlook should define objectivity. God's view should provide the objective meaning of history.

So how do we get God's view of history? Who can scale the heavens to bring God down? We can't, of course. But since God chose to come down and reveal himself and his purposes to us, we might be able to find what the Greek historians and philosophers despaired of ever finding—that is, the basis for a universal history.

The pagans knew that they could not have a science without universal principles. But universal principles were elusive because no one could transcend his own culture—and no one dared to question the rightness of the regime.

Not until the Bible do we encounter histories written by historical losers. God's people were regularly defeated, enslaved, oppressed, occupied, and exiled. Yet they told their story honestly, because they held themselves—and their historians—to a higher judgment, higher even than the king or the forces of the market. They looked at history in terms of God's judgment, blessings, curses, and mercy. This became their principle of selection and interpretation of events. It didn't matter so much whether the story flattered the king or the victorious armies.

The Bible's human authors saw history in terms of covenant. In the ancient world, a covenant was the sacred and legal way that people created a family bond. Marriage was a covenant, and adoption was a covenant. And God's relationship with his people was always based on a covenant.

God's plan for the kingdom of heaven uses the kingdoms of earth. And these kingdoms are engaged by God and evangelized for his purpose. Providence harnesses the road system and the political system of the Roman Empire, and puts it all to use to advance the Gospel. Yet Rome, too, came in for divine judgment. If God did not spare the holy city of Jerusalem, then neither would Rome be exempted.

And so the pattern continued through all the subsequent thousands of years—through the rise and fall of the Byzantine Empire, the European empires, and into the new world order that exists for our own fleeting moment.

There's a danger, of course, in trying to discern God's perspective. We run the risk of moralizing, presuming too much, or playing the prophet. There's always a danger, too, of identifying God with one "side" or another in a given war or rivalry. Christian history, at its best, transcends these problems. We can recognize that even when pagan Persia was the most vehement enemy of Christian Byzantium, the tiny Christian minority in Persia was practicing the most pure and refined Christianity the world has seen. When God uses imperial structures to advance the Gospel, the imperial structures have no monopoly on God.

It takes a subtle, discerning, and modest hand to write truly Christian history. In studying world events, a Christian historian must strive to see God's fatherly plan for the whole human race and how it has unfolded since the first Pentecost.

Christian history tells the story not of an empire, nor of a culture, but of a family. And it is a story, not a scientific treatise. In many languages, the connection is clear. In Spanish, Portuguese, Italian, and German, for example, the same word is used for "history" as for "story": *historia, história, storia, Geschichte*. In English we can lose sight of this and teach history as a succession of dates to be memorized and maps to be drawn. The time lines and atlases are certainly important, but they don't communicate to ordinary people why they should want to read history. Jacques Barzun complained, almost a half century ago, that history had fallen out of usefulness for ordinary people and was little read. It had fragmented into overspecialized microdisciplines, with off-putting names like "psychohistory" and "quantohistory."

The authors in this series strive to communicate history in a way that's accessible and even entertaining. They see history as true stories well told. They don't fear humor or pathos as threats to their trustworthiness. They are unabashed about their chosen perspective, but they are neither producing propaganda nor trashing tradition. The sins and errors of Christians (even Christian saints) are an important part of the grand narrative.

The Catholic Church's story is our inheritance, our legacy, our pride and joy, and our cautionary tale. We ignore the past at our peril. We cannot see the present clearly without a deep sense of Christian history.

Mike Aquilina
Reclaiming Catholic History Series Editor

Chronology of
The Church and the Middle Ages
(1000–1378)

1009	Destruction of the Church of the Holy Sepulchre in Jerusalem
1049–1054	Pontificate of St. Leo IX
1054	The Great Schism
1059	Pope Nicholas II decree on papal election by College of Cardinals
1066	Battle of Hastings
1071	Battle of Manzikert
1072	Death of St. Peter Damian
1073–1085	Pontificate of Pope St. Gregory VII
1077	The Confession at Canossa
1095	Pope Bl. Urban II begins crusading movement
1096–1102	First Crusade
1099	Liberation of Jerusalem by crusaders
1123	First Lateran Council
1139	Second Lateran Council
1147–1149	Second Crusade
1153	Death of St. Bernard of Clairvaux
1170	Murder of St. Thomas Becket in Canterbury Cathedral

1170–1221   St. Dominic

1179   Third Lateran Council

1181–1226   St. Francis of Assisi

1187   Battle of Hattin and loss of Jerusalem

1189–1192   Third Crusade

1198–1216   Pontificate of Innocent III

1201–1205   Fourth Crusade

1204   Sack of Constantinople by crusaders

1209–1229   Albigensian Crusade

1215   Fourth Lateran Council

1218–1221   Fifth Crusade

1228–1229   "Crusade" of Frederick II

1231   Establishment of procedures for medieval inquisitors by Pope Gregory IX

1242–1248   Construction of Sainte Chapelle in Paris

1245   First Council of Lyons

1248–1254   First Crusade of King St. Louis IX of France

1269–1272   Second Crusade of King St. Louis IX of France

1274   Second Council of Lyons; deaths of Sts. Bonaventure and Thomas Aquinas

1291   Fall of Acre: Last Christian stronghold in the Latin East

1294   Abdication of Pope St. Celestine V

1294–1303   Pontificate of Boniface VIII

1309–1378   Papal residence in Avignon, France

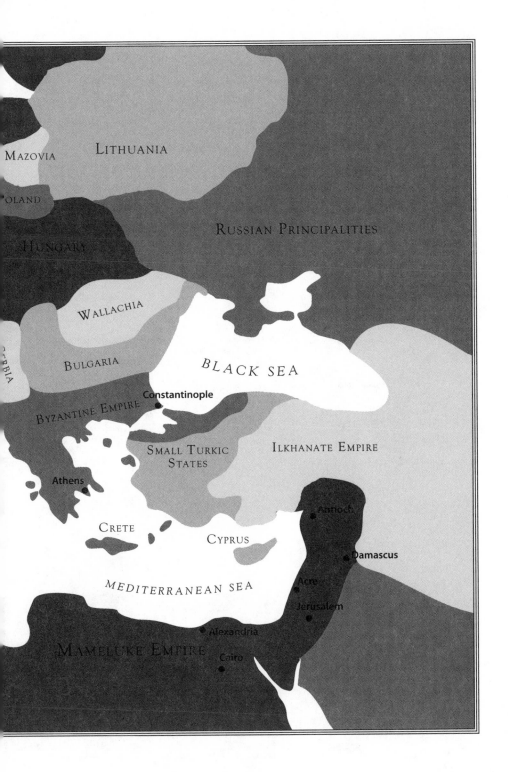

Introduction

What's in a Name?

W hy is it that we mainly remember the Middle Ages by absurd things? When we talk of something medieval, we mean something quaint. We remember that alchemy was medieval, or that heraldry was medieval. We forget that Parliaments are medieval, that all our Universities are medieval, that city corporations are medieval, that gunpowder and printing are medieval, that half the things by which we now live, and to which we look for progress, are medieval.

—*G. K. Chesterton*[1]

No one living in the eleventh through the fourteenth centuries believed they were in the "Middle Ages." Indeed, German historians identified the years covered by the term when compiling medieval source documents.[2] Labeling historical time periods is a convention of scholars in an effort to organize human events into a definable and digestible configuration. The use of time periods to define history often produces raucous debate within the scholarly community. Periodization can be useful for pedagogical methods in an educational environment, but it can also be misleading and lead to false narratives that persist for centuries. Take, for instance, the commonly used word *medieval* to describe the centuries covered in this book. The term has a circuitous history with origins in the seventeenth century. Derived from the Latin words *medium* and *aevum* (middle ages), the word was originally intended as an insult, indicating the years between the ancient and modern worlds were nothing special.

It is not rare for "modern" historians, armed with a sense of supe-riority, to create words and phrases describing the past that are more a commentary on the prejudice of modernity than an accurate repre-sentation of past ages of human experience.[3] That's why it is no surprise that Protestant authors used the term *medieval* to disparage the Church, and Enlightenment authors solidified the modern understanding of the word as a synonym for *barbaric, bloody, superstitious, primitive, bigoted,* and *intolerant,* among others.[4] These thinkers believed the Middle Ages were, at best, a time of darkness suffocating human advancement and, at worst, the age of an overbearing, omnipotent Catholic Church bent on controlling minds and hearts with superstitious nonsense.

As a result, some historians argue the term should be abandoned not only for the associated negativity but also because the term encompasses a period (usually identified as 500–1500) too clumsy and too generic for useful study. Instead of discarding the term, perhaps it is time to change the negative undertones associated with it and see the medieval period for what it was: a time of penetrating activity in multiple areas of human life rooted in the knowledge of a loving and merciful God in whom human civilization and culture find their ultimate meaning and purpose. The story of the Church during these "glory years" is one of intense faith, grandiose adventures, and brilliant advancements in human achievement. Notwithstanding centuries of misrepresentation, the actions of the faith-ful men and women of this period and their accomplishments reverberate to the modern day.

Chapter 1

Medieval Man
in a Medieval World

F or three long centuries . . . society enjoyed what
may be considered the richest, most fruitful,
most harmonious epoch in all the history of
Europe, an epoch which may be likened to spring after
the barbarian winter.

—*Henri Daniel-Rops*[1]

Catholic historian Warren H. Carroll (1932–2011) termed the centuries
covered in this book the "Glory of Christendom."[2] While medieval man
might not have known he was living in the "Middle Ages," he understood
the reality of the term *Christendom*. The popes were the primary users of
the term and expanded its definition through the centuries. Pope John
VIII (r. 872–882) utilized the word *Christiantias* to signify the common
interests of all Christians in the temporal sphere. Usually Christendom
meant a spiritual reality inhabited by all baptized Christians and not a
specific geographic area, although Pope St. Gregory VII (r. 1073–1085)
used it to mean the temporal territory inhabited by Christians. Bl. Urban
II (r. 1088–1099) centered the meaning of Christendom on the unity of
believers motivated by a common goal for the good of Christ and the
Church. The ultimate definition of Christendom came from Innocent III
(r. 1198–1216), who used the word to describe the true society of Christian states girded by the precepts of the Gospel and supremely ruled by
the Vicar of Christ, the Roman pontiff.[3]

Secular and ecclesial authorities were separate in Christendom but theoretically united for common temporal interests and spiritually focused on assisting each citizen to attain eternal life. The reality was, however, far from the theory. Although there were monarchs who viewed themselves as protectors of the Church, there were also secular rulers who sought to control the Church and use it for their own political agendas. The tension between Church and state in Christendom is one of the main characters in the story of the Church during the Middle Ages. Although there was no Christendom without the Church, the reverse was not true as the Church was distinct from Christendom. Occasionally, popes forgot or ignored that distinction, and the result was times of great distress and discomfort for the Bride of Christ.

The Medieval Worldview

No study of the Middle Ages can occur without recognition of the worldview of those who lived during its years. Those who are quick to view the past from a position of supposed superiority come to erroneous conclusions. Understanding historical events from a contemporary perspective provides greater insight into why people made the decisions they did and allows a more accurate representation and understanding of their choices. Today, people often struggle to comprehend the Middle Ages, not only because of false narratives perpetuated by the media (nearly every movie set in the Middle Ages portrays life as brutish, dirty, and depressing), but also because the medieval worldview is vastly different from—even incompatible with— our modern or postmodern perspective. This is most clearly seen in the two principles on which medieval society was centered: hierarchy and faith.

Medieval society was hierarchical, which, by its nature, is unequal and authoritative. Democracy as a form of societal government was nonexistent. Modern industrialization and its concomitant aspects were not present; medieval society was rooted in the land and centered on agricultural work. Medieval people recognized and accepted class stratification and its authoritative nature, which was enforced through violent means at times but mostly through societal norms and values.[4] At the top of medieval society was the king. The Englishman John of Salisbury (1115/20–1180), a student of the famous medieval thinker Peter Abelard and secretary to the martyr St. Thomas Becket, illustrated the medieval view of kings in his twelfth-century work *Policraticus*: "The place of the head in the body of the commonwealth is filled by the prince, who is subject only to God and to those who exercise His office and represent Him on earth, even as in the human body the head is quickened and governed by the soul."[5]

Despite his lofty position, the medieval king did not exercise absolute control over all aspects of his realm. He is best described as an overlord of other lords. There were medieval monarchs who tried to acquire absolute power, but other nobles and the Church frequently checked their plans. Indeed, the thirteenth-century author of the German document *Schwabenspiegel* aptly described medieval mentality concerning hierarchical authority: "We should serve our lords for they protect us; if they do not protect us, justice does not oblige us to serve them."[6] Despite the nonabsolute power exercised by kings, they were accorded special authority and responsibilities.

Medieval man was a thoroughly religious being, and the key to understanding the medieval world lies with the Catholic faith. The Church and its sacraments imbued all aspects of medieval society. The Catholic faith provided medieval society with a common way of life, a common purpose, and unity. The centrality of the Catholic faith in the medieval world is illustrated by the story of the vicious warrior who was confronted by a bishop for his sins. The warrior cried out, "Give me absolution or I'll kill you." The stalwart bishop offered his neck to the man and said, "Strike!" Dumbfounded by the resolute manner of the cleric, the soldier hesitated and then replied, "No. I don't like you well enough to send you straight to heaven!"[7] Despite his sins, the warrior recognized he needed absolution from the Church as the instrument of mercy and salvation in the world. Additionally, he believed in martyrdom and the reality of eternity. This story is not to suggest that the medieval world was full of saintliness and

harmony (although those elements were definitely present in it). Human
sinfulness and conflict were as present then as they are now. Still, the story
is emblematic of the value medieval people placed on the Catholic Church
and its teachings. The faith unified European medieval society in a way
that is incomprehensible to us, and that partly explains the persistence of
myths and misconceptions about this time period.

Feudalism

Just as the term *Middle Ages* is debated among medieval historians, the term
feudalism and its meaning have been the subject of intense discussion within
the scholarly community.[8] The standard historical narrative posits that as
the Carolingian political structures (in what is today France, Belgium, the
Netherlands, Austria, and parts of Germany) ended in the middle tenth
century, a new political system cemented in the acquisition and control of
land emerged. Most of us know this new political system as feudalism, which
was not a term used in the medieval period but rather a construct used by
Renaissance Italian jurists in the sixteenth century to describe customary
laws of property. Feudalism "denotes the grant of income-producing property (usually land), known as the benefice or fief, by the lord and protector
in return for the promise of oath of fealty by the vassal."[9]

The invasions and attacks of Islamic, Magyar, and Viking warriors
spawned the need for protection, as the standard narrative posits, which was
granted at the price of "subordination, subjection, and dependence."[10] Society divided into those who needed protection and those who provided it.
Certain warriors controlled large areas of land, and in order to administer
them properly, they parceled land to other warriors in exchange for military
aid, counsel and advice, and a percentage of the fruits of the property. Feudalism was not a perfect system, nor was it uniformly practiced throughout
Christendom (in fact, it was not practiced at all in some places).[11]

The central element of feudal society was the oath that was given in a
ceremony initially known as commendation and then as homage. Medieval society was rooted in personal relationships; the oath bound one man

to another. The most important relationship was between a lord (grantor of the benefice or fief) and vassal (grantee). Generally, the vassal owed military service (before the twelfth century, this was true only in England), which amounted to forty days annually, in exchange for the fief and the lord's protection. Some historians argue not that medieval people were focused on this commonly portrayed "lord and vassal" relationship but rather that they functioned through multiple types of relationships, such as "ruler and subject, patron and client, landlord and tenant, employer and employed, commander and soldier."[12]

The medieval world was a primarily agricultural society, so land was the main commodity. Superiors provided land to subordinates in exchange for fealty, rents, and labor. The granting of fiefs began when the Church provided lands to noblemen as a means to protect Church property. A nobleman holding ecclesial land was responsible for its protection and upkeep. Initially, fiefs were held for life and not hereditary; they became inheritable over time. Although the modern academic community debates the utility of the terms *feudalism, fief,* and *vassal,* they are useful constructs when specifically defined and applied to the appropriate areas of Europe to explain the societal and political structures in place in medieval Christendom.[13]

The Three Orders of Medieval Society

Class-stratified medieval Europe consisted of "those who prayed, those who fought, and those who worked."[14] Medieval man knew his place in the world and usually did not seek to upset the well-established societal order. Movement between the classes was usually limited, but not within the Church. The Catholic Church provided a place of opportunity for those who demonstrated tenacity and skill despite their class background. It was possible for the son of a serf or an artisan to rise to the highest offices in the Church.

Nobles and Knights

The nobility comprised those who had the means to purchase weapons, the time to train with them, and the willingness to use them. Nobles had the ability to buy, train, and use weapons because they lived off the work of other people. Noblemen were expected to follow a code of honor, known as chivalry, which was rooted in Christian behavior such as Mass attendance, penitential practices, just conduct in war, and the protection of widows, orphans, and the Church.

A distinctive element of noble life, which was tied to the notions of chivalry, involved the idea of courtly love and the role of the troubadour. Marriage for the nobility was a political and economic decision more than a romantic or personal one. The decision of whom to marry was often at the discretion of not the bride or groom but rather their parents. Although some noble marriages were successful with both parties remaining faithful, extramarital affairs were very common. Noble courtly love expressed in the vernacular, usually in the form of poems, became an outlet for the strict confines of noble marriage. The object of courtly love was usually a married woman, whom the nobleman adored and to whom he professed his undying love. These popular poems were performed in noble courts by troubadours (from the French *trouver*, "to find"), usually knights (although some were clerics and from the middle class) who expressed the stories of courtly love through song. The first known troubadour was the knight Duke William IX of Aquitaine (1071–1127).

The Western knight appears in history in the ninth and tenth centuries, reaches his zenith in the eleventh through the thirteen centuries, and declines beginning in the fourteenth century.[15] The process of becoming a knight began at the age of fourteen when noble boys became squires and assisted knights in their daily activities. When the boy had apprenticed for years and was ready to take on the responsibilities of knighthood, a ceremony was conducted. The young man took an oath to embody the chivalric values and was handed his sword, which had been blessed by a cleric with a special prayer:

> Hear, O Lord, our petitions and bless with thy majestic hand
> this sword wherewith thy servant desires to be girt, so that he
> may be enabled both to defend churches, widows, orphans, and
> all servants of God against the cruelty of pagans, and also to
> strike fear into the hearts of traitors.[16]

Originally, any knight could make someone else a knight, but in the early twelfth century, knighthood was closed to anyone not related to a knight (in the areas of Europe outside England).

When not engaged in active war, knights trained for war by participating in tournaments. Actual medieval tournaments were very different from the reenactments at modern-day *Medieval Times* restaurants and fairs. They were large-scale, multiday events encompassing wide areas of territory involving, at times, hundreds of knights. Tournaments were nasty, bloody affairs with "few rules and no referees."[17] Injury and death were common outcomes, and as such, the Church in the twelfth century banned participation in tournaments at the local councils of Clermont (1130) and Reims (1131), and at the ecumenical council of Second Lateran (1139).[18] Despite the Church's ban, however, tournaments remained popular events and provided a meaningful training opportunity for knights, whose primary function in medieval society was ensuring peace through readiness and training in martial skills.

Castles

The limited competency of medieval government led to the creation of strongholds that served as homes for the nobility, centers of estate administration, and protection from invasions and armed attacks. The castle served the military purposes of defense and functioned as a base from which to conduct military operations in the surrounding countryside. The first castles in the early tenth century were known as "motte-and-bailey" constructions. They consisted of a wooden (and later stone) keep (nobleman's house) on a raised mound of dirt (motte) with an enclosed courtyard (bailey) protected by a ditch or wooden palisade. Toward the end of the tenth century, castle construction switched to stone, which provided stronger protection from attack and was far less vulnerable to fire than wood. Castles were originally rectangular in shape, but that design allowed sappers to destroy the corners easily (round towers at the end of walls were much more difficult to undermine). Castles were expensive to build and maintain and required extensive manpower for defense as well as for everyday use. A castle household consisted of military personnel, such as knights, men-at-arms, watchmen, and guards, as well as the domestic staff of servants.

Up Close and Personal:
ABBOT SUGER OF ST. DENIS (CA. 1081–1151)

Abbot Suger was the son of a serf and yet rose to occupy the most powerful nonroyal position in the kingdom of France. He was an ambitious man who desired to bolster the power of the French king and glorify God through the beautification and enrichment of the royal abbey of St. Denis. Suger studied at the abbey school with the future Louis VI, "the Fat" (r. 1108–1137), and they became lifelong friends. He was also an advisor to Louis VII (r. 1137–1180) and served as regent during the king's absence while participating in the Second Crusade (1147–1149). Despite his resistance to the king's crusade expedition, Suger faithfully governed the realm in Louis's absence and was rewarded for his actions when Louis named him "Father of the Country."

Suger became abbot at St. Denis in 1122 and held the position nearly thirty years before his death. He initiated a monastic reform at the abbey spurred by a reprimand from St. Bernard of Clairvaux. Bernard chastised Suger for his lax and worldly focus and behavior by telling him to "live as a monk serving God as minister of his king, rather than as a minister who, by chance, happened to be a Benedictine" (quoted in Daniel-Rops, *Cathedral and Crusade*, 96–97). As part of the reform, Suger undertook a major renovation of the abbey church at St. Denis and wrote a book (*On the Abbey Church of St.-Denis and Its Art Treasures*) detailing the construction efforts. In one humorous story, Suger recounts how his builders said that trees tall enough to provide the length he wanted for the roof did not exist. Suger decided to take the skeptical carpenters into the woods, wherein he found twelve trees of the required length and ordered them cut and hauled to the building site. Suger was consumed with beauty and considered it an earthly reflection of God. His architectural revolution at St. Denis sparked an international building campaign directed to the glory of God for centuries and provides an example of the ingenuity and faithfulness of medieval Christians. Suger was short in stature, but his impact on Western civilization was immense, as his friend Simon Chèvre d'Or remarked in an obituary: "He refused in his smallness, to be a small man" (Simon Chèvre d'Or, quoted in Abbot Suger, *On the Abbey Church of St.–Denis and Its Art Treasures*, 33).

The Serf

Knights and the nobility occupied the higher end of medieval society, and at the lower end were peasants who worked the land. These agricultural workers and craftsmen (smiths, carpenters, millers, tanners, etc.) were divided into those who were free and those who were not. A freeman held land without the labor obligation due to a nobleman. They rode horses and carried swords but were not trained in the military arts. Nonfree peasants or serfs (also known as *villeins*) owed service on the lord's land (known as the *demesne*), which usually amounted to two-thirds of their time. Serfs could not leave the land or sell livestock without the lord's permission and were subject to the payment of fees for various activities. The work was hard and demanding, but medieval society followed the Church calendar, which provided for rest from work on Sundays, holy days, and various saints' feasts.

The Medieval Village

The foundation of life in medieval Europe was the village. Medieval peasants were well aware of their village's boundaries and related to other people based on their village of residence. The village was a community ordered for agricultural production and centered on a monastery, church, or a manor house (the lord's estate).[19] A typical medieval English village comprised communal space such as the village green, a shared oven for bread, open fields, and public and private buildings. Pigs were the most numerous livestock, along with cows, which were used to breed oxen for the plows, and sheep and goats, which were used primarily for milk and cheese. The staple crops were barley, oats, and rye. Wheat was grown and harvested as the cash crop to pay rents and taxes.[20] Overseeing the lord's estate was the steward (also known as the *seneschal*), who acted as the lord's deputy and inspected the village several times a year to report on its productivity. The day-to-day manager of the estate, acting as the chief law officer and business manager, was the bailiff. The lord entrusted the oversight of the estate to these men and rarely interacted with the villagers. Peasant homes were made of wood and straw and housed both human and animal occupants. Food was sometimes scarce but consisted mostly of grains and cooked fruit; protein consumption was usually insufficient. On days of rest, the peasant enjoyed various forms of recreation, including board games like chess, checkers, backgammon, and rolling dice. Physical activity such as wrestling, swimming, and archery were common pastimes. The most ubiquitous recreation was drinking ale, which was brewed, usually by women, in large quantities. Village life was hard, but there were opportunities to enjoy life. The village provided the majority of medieval people a place of employment, recreation, and relative safety.

The Medieval City

Although villages were the most numerous local communal structures in medieval Europe, towns and cities increased in number and population during this period as well. Most major medieval cities had originated as centers of imperial Roman administration, and then became centers of Church administration with the collapse of central imperial government in the late fifth century. Medieval cities were hubs of commerce; many held popular fairs where merchants from across Christendom gathered to hawk their wares. Some areas became centers of education with the creation of universities.

At the beginning of the Middle Ages, there were only a handful of cities with a population over ten thousand, but with technological advances in agriculture, including the moldboard plow, the horse collar, and the three-field system of crop rotation,[21] European population significantly increased (indeed, it tripled between the years 950 and 1300).[22] As population increased overall, so did the inhabitants of towns and cities. The *Domesday Book*, compiled at the order of William the Conqueror in 1086, showed that 10 percent of England's 1.1 million people lived in towns. By the end of the twelfth century, London's population had increased to eighty thousand people. Cities on the Continent were even more populated; Paris and Milan combined boasted two hundred thousand inhabitants in the year 1300, and Florence, Venice, and Genoa were home to one hundred thousand citizens.[23] As towns and cities grew in population and technological advances helped increase the agricultural yield, the movement of goods and people increased as well. Significant changes in social and economic structures occurred from the beginning to the end of the medieval period, which affected medieval life in both positive and negative ways.

The Church in the Middle Ages

The Catholic Church was a vibrant and central institution in the medieval period. The Church had not merely survived the collapse of central imperial governing authority from Rome in the late fifth century but actually thrived. As European social and political systems changed in the years after the Western empire's collapse, the Church remained the only organized multinational institution in the West. As such, it was the Church and its monks who formed a bulwark against the potential loss of Western civilization and culture.

The Church's influence was widespread, partially because European culture was imbued with Christian virtues and principles, but also because of the number of clerics and religious men and women. While there was no vocations crisis in terms of numbers of clerics, there were certainly times of widespread clerical formation issues, such as the promise of celibacy, which was not always authentically lived. Although medieval society was highly class stratified, the Church allowed for upward mobility. One's ability and fidelity mattered more than one's parentage.

Catholic medieval life was rooted in the parish. The parish priest served as the Church's main agent in the lives of medieval people. He alone baptized children, witnessed marriages, and conducted funerals. The faithful were obliged to attend Mass at their parish (the modern idea of going to whatever Mass fits the family schedule was completely alien to medieval people). This obligation was considered serious enough that the archbishop of Bordeaux threatened excommunication for any priest who allowed nonparishioners to worship at his parish![24]

The Church's influence was significant in the medieval period partly due to its extensive and organized bureaucracy. The medieval papacy maintained central authority through papal legates who served as representatives of the Roman pontiff in royal courts and secular governments. The Church's administration comprised an independent court system with its own law, judges, lawyers, and prisons. One source of tension between Church and state was the exclusive jurisdiction of ecclesial courts over clerics and religious. This legal prerogative incensed some secular rulers. Ecclesiastical courts and jails were known as more just and efficient than their secular counterparts. There are cases of criminals in secular jail committing ecclesial crimes (such as blasphemy or heresy) in order to move to a Church jail.

Another source of friction between Church and state concerned finances. The pope received large sums of money from the Papal States (his large temporal landholdings in central Italy), the Peter's Pence collection (income from those lands subject in authority to the papacy), fees from churches and monasteries directly dependent on Rome, pallium fees (a pallium is a special stole given to archbishops), fees for bulls (documents affixed with the papal seal), indulgences and dispensations, and gifts of land from laymen. As the Church's wealth grew over time, envious secular rulers designed ways to confiscate Church wealth for their own purposes.

Prayer and Worship

The cult of saints was strong in medieval society and manifested itself in great devotions, prayers of intercession, and pilgrimages. The veneration of relics occupied a prime place in medieval spirituality, especially any relics associated with the Lord's agony, passion, and death, as well as any related to the Blessed Mother. Medieval Christians believed in the reality of miracles and supernatural intervention in human affairs. They were familiar with sacred scripture—especially the gospels. Hand-copied vernacular editions of the Bible and prayer books were widespread for the literate. For the illiterate, paintings, sculptures, and stained glass containing scenes from scripture were used. The Church's sacraments were an integral part of medieval life, especially the sacrament of Confession, which was very popular. Medieval Catholics were acutely aware of their sinfulness, and armed with contrition, most desired to perform penances to demonstrate forgiveness, conversion, and satisfaction. The Eucharist, however, was received rarely; even pious persons received the Eucharist only a handful of times a year. The practice of infrequent reception of Communion was the result of humility and great reverence for the gift of Christ himself under the appearance of wine and bread. Medieval people did not want to commit sacrilege, so they hesitated to receive the Eucharist frequently; when they did receive, it was after diligent preparation.[25]

YOU BE THE JUDGE:

Were serfs slaves?

One major myth about the Middle Ages concerns the status of serfs. On the one hand, some insist on presenting serfs as though they were the equivalent of slaves. On the other hand, the French medievalist Régine Pernoud recalled how French schoolchildren were taught that the serfs spent the majority of their time beating ponds with sticks to quiet the frogs so the lord could sleep (*Those Terrible Middle Ages: Debunking the Myths*, 89)! Neither of these extreme views is correct.

Since the Church was a dominant actor in medieval society, some historians criticize the Church for allowing widespread slavery in apparent contravention of Gospel precepts. There is little basis for that. The Church had long experience with the evils of slavery as it was born into the world of imperial Rome, which was largely founded on the institution of slavery. After the collapse of central governing authority from Rome in the late fifth century, the Church's influence in European society increased, and as a result, the institution of slavery was no longer present in the medieval period. Serfs were never considered the property of their lord in medieval society; they were treated as people, not property. Unlike slaves, serfs had a right to marry and have a family. In addition, their tenure on the land (a small parcel set aside for their personal use) could be passed down to an heir. Although the work was arduous, the peasant received nearly a hundred days of rest annually due to the holy days and feasts on the Church's liturgical calendar. Societal mechanisms were also in place to allow for the serfs to be free from working on the lord's lands under certain conditions, such as participation in a crusade. Serfs were allowed to volunteer for a crusade without their lord's permission, and the act of "taking the cross" provided the serf's freedom. Serfs who left their land for the allure of the town were recognized as free after a stay of one year and a day. Beginning in the later twelfth century, kings demanded the freedom of serfs for economic reasons. Serfs paid taxes and performed services for local lords and nobility. Kings desired greater control of their realm and realized the payment of royal taxes to the local lord first provided opportunities for skimming and cheating. In order to increase the royal coffers, kings advocated for the freedom of serfs. The Church advocated for the freedom of serfs as well. So, despite the myths, serfdom was not a medieval form of slavery but an entirely different and unique social construct of the Middle Ages.

The Cathedrals

Perhaps the most grandiose expression of medieval spirituality was the construction of the magnificent cathedrals, still standing centuries later as permanent reminders of the love of Christ, the saints, and the Church exhibited by the Christians who built them. Church architecture borrowed heavily from Roman designs in the centuries after imperial legalization. The Roman basilica with its long nave, aisles divided by columns, and a covered wooden roof was the model for Christian churches. After the collapse of imperial power in the West, a new style of architecture, known as Romanesque, emerged. This style used thick walls, narrow windows (which limited the amount of light in the building), and wooden roofs of limited height, which were heavily susceptible to fire hazard.

Near the turn of the eleventh century, a new architectural style emerged, one that produced some of the most glorious monuments ever created. This revolutionary architectural style originated with the royal abbey church of St. Denis near Paris, which contained the relics of its namesake, the beheaded third-century bishop martyr who evangelized Paris and the surrounding region. King Dagobert I, king of all the Franks (r. 629–634), founded the abbey church and was the first of many French monarchs to be buried there.

The architectural innovation in the construction of sacred buildings involved increasing the height of the walls in order to provide more room for windows, which produced more light and allowed for a heightened sense of raising a person's gaze and aspirations toward heaven. A feature of the new architectural style was ribbed rather than barrel vaulting. While the ribbed vault allowed for an increase in wall height and interior space, it also placed significant pressure on the walls. French architects and engineers countered the outward thrust of the walls by creating the "flying buttress," which became the distinctive characteristic of these new cathedrals. The new style gave the building a sense of soaring toward heaven, which was ironic given the significant downward thrust.[26] The new style was later termed *Gothic* by Italians during the Renaissance but is perhaps more appropriately called the *French* style.[27]

Cathedral building was a social undertaking as a town's populace frequently provided the manpower required to build the massive structures. The inhabitants of Chartres in 1144 harnessed themselves to carts in order to deliver stone to the construction site, and people from the surrounding countryside brought food and supplies for the builders.[28] The French took their cathedral building seriously, and by the mid-thirteenth century there were fifty cathedrals under construction.[29] Cathedral building defined the Middle Ages as the new style spread from France throughout Christendom. It was an expression of the deep and vibrant faith of medieval people as well as a testament to their intellectual ingenuity and physical strength.

Chapter 2

The Papal Reform Movement Begins

T he Church shall be Catholic, chaste and free: Catholic in the faith and fellowship of the saints, chaste from all contagion of evil and free from secular power.

—*Bl. Pope Urban II*[1]

Assuaging a guilty conscience for committing a murder in a youthful rage, Duke William of Aquitaine (875–918) founded the monastery of Cluny in the early years of the tenth century. The duke desired prayers for his soul and chose a reform-minded monk, Berno (d. 927), as first abbot of the monastery. Berno enforced a strict adherence to the Rule of St. Benedict so that Cluny would not be another lax and worldly monastery.

Monasteries were usually subject to the authority of the local bishop during the later Roman Empire, but with its collapse in the late fifth century, local secular rulers sought to control monasteries, which were economic engines and sources of great wealth. As a result, Duke William knew his monastic establishment might not fulfill his desires if left unprotected from the encroachment of his political successors and the local bishop, so he made an unusual request for papal protection of the Cluny monks in the foundation document:

> These monks should not be subjected to my own rule, nor that of my relatives, nor that of the king, nor that of any other power on earth. No secular prince, no count, no bishop, nor the pope

> himself shall invade the property of these servants of God, or
> alienate it, diminish it, exchange it, give it a benefice to any-
> one, or set any ruler over it against their will. And in order to
> ensure that rash and wicked men never succeed in carrying out
> such a blasphemous act, I call upon the pope himself . . . to use
> the canonical and apostolic authority given to him by God to
> excommunicate . . . any robbers, invaders, and thieves of these
> possessions which I am so readily surrendering.[2]

Holiness attracts, and the arduous spiritual practices of the monks at
Cluny stood in stark contrast to the immorality widely practiced by clergy
and monks during the tenth century. The pope sent Odo (d. 942), Berno's successor as abbot, on a monastic reform mission, which succeeded
in uniting several monasteries to Cluny. By the beginning of the twelfth
century, there were nearly a thousand monasteries under Cluny's authority, making the abbot of the famous monastery one of the most influential churchmen of the day. Cluny's influence reached the highest levels
of Church hierarchy as four of its members rose to the Chair of St. Peter,
three in the eleventh century alone.[3] When he founded it, Duke William
had no idea his establishment of Cluny would provide Christendom with
the instruments for a great Church reform that was desperately needed as
the eleventh century dawned.

The Papal Reform Program

By the midpoint of the eleventh century, the Church suffered from the
evils of simony (the buying and selling of Church offices) and violations
of clerical celibacy. These sins had reached such a level of significant crisis
that only a radical program of reform could restore the Church. Authentic
reform had to start at the top with popes committed to fully implement-
ing the reform initiatives.

Providentially, holy monks, men who were free from the contagions
of simony, corruption, and sexual immorality, were elected as pope. These
men brought the reform initiatives from their monasteries to the universal

Church. Cluny was the most important of these monasteries, but not the only one. The Italian reformer St. William of Volpiano (960–1031) established a series of reform monasteries in Normandy. Another Norman reform monastery was founded at Bec, by the ex-warrior-turned-monk Herluin; it also became a premier center of scholarship in Christendom. The reform popes implemented new policies, removed unworthy bishops and clergy, and reorganized the Roman curia (papal court). Because they were in need of faithful and loyal servants and emissaries, these popes relied more heavily on the cardinals. Originally, the title *cardinal* was applied to priests of principal churches throughout Christendom, but it came to be associated with a select group in the city of Rome. In Rome, the term had been used for the deacons of the city's seven administrative regions. These cardinals assisted at papal liturgies, performed administrative tasks, and distributed alms to the poor. In the early medieval period, bishops of the surrounding area near Rome were given the title *cardinal*. They assisted the pope with ecclesiastical affairs, often representing him as legates at synods and other gatherings. The number of cardinals varied throughout the medieval period, but there were usually fifty or so. During the eleventh-century papal reform movement, the cardinals gained greater prominence and authority. Before delving into the details of the reform, it is important to understand why a reform was needed in the first place.

The Curious Pontificate(s) of Benedict IX

By the end of the tenth century, the papacy had become mired in a game of regional and international politics and was seen as a commodity that could be bought and sold by local Roman aristocratic families. The choice of papal candidates reflected this sad state of affairs as no pope in the tenth century was recognized as a saint. Indeed, there was nearly a 170-year gap in papal saints!

Illustrative of this period is the curious case of Benedict IX. After a three-year pontificate, Sergius IV died in 1012, and the fight to determine his successor was carried out by two rival Italian families. After losing a

literal street fight in Rome, one family sought the intervention of Henry
II, the king of the Germans. He established their candidate, Benedict VIII
(r. 1012–1024), on the throne in exchange for the imperial title *emperor.*
The family kept the papacy and several years later once more mandated
the election of one of its members, and so Benedict IX (r. 1032–1044: 1045;
1047–1048), nephew of the previous two popes, was elected. In order to
secure his election, Benedict IX used a large amount of money provided by
his father, Count Alberic III. Benedict IX was the epitome of the immoral
popes of the age. He was a young man of twenty who lived a debauched
lifestyle, and "with him the papacy became an object of needed reform
rather than the source of it."[4]

In 1044, the Roman people became weary of Benedict's wickedness
and forced him from the city. They elected an antipope, Sylvester III, who
"reigned" for less than two months before Benedict returned to the city
in triumph. Shortly thereafter, however, Benedict tired of the papacy and
its demands. Likely desirous of marriage (allegedly to his cousin), Benedict IX abdicated the papacy on March 1, 1045—on the condition he was
reimbursed the funds used to procure the papacy.

The popular, well-known, and holy priest John Gratian replaced him,
taking the name Gregory VI (r. 1045–1046). Although John (Gregory VI)
desired to return the papacy to its holy function and saintly reformers supported him, he committed simony when he raised a large sum of money
to reimburse Benedict. Gregory VI inherited a Rome in virtual anarchy
with no effective government. He instituted reforms and appointed the
holy monk Hildebrand to form an armed guard for the protection of the
city and the Church's property, especially pilgrimage shrines. Despite
Gregory's positive achievements, news of his simony became public knowledge and support for his pontificate waned. In the meantime, Benedict
IX regretted his decision to abdicate the papacy and returned to Rome in
1046 demanding his reinstatement.

The fiasco of three men claiming the papacy (Benedict IX, Gregory
VI, and the antipope Sylvester III) forced secular intervention in the form
of Henry III, king of the Germans. Henry, a pious and just ruler, who

recognized the need for Church reform, held a synod at the town of Sutri (about an hour's drive northwest of Rome) in December 1046. At the synod, Gregory VI consented to abdicate the papacy due to his simony. Benedict IX's and Sylvester III's claims to the papacy were not recognized. The king then nominated a new pope, the German bishop Sudiger, who was elected by the Roman clergy, acclaimed by the people, and took the name Clement II (r. 1046–1047). The newly consecrated pope crowned Henry III emperor on Christmas Day 1046.

The curious tale of Benedict IX was not over, however. He refused to recognize the king's decision at Sutri and returned to Rome in November 1047 upon the death of Clement II. His final "term" as pope was a short stint, less than a year, before he was forced out of Rome once more and replaced by another German bishop, who took the name Damasus II (r. 1048). The end of Benedict's days remains shrouded in mystery. There are tales he died believing he was still pope. Other stories indicate he retired to the abbey of Grottaferrata, a short distance south of Rome, where he rejected the claim to the papacy and lived his remaining days in penance. Regardless, his pontificate(s) clearly showed the need for Church reform and particularly the end of secular interference, especially in choosing the successor of Peter.

The Election of the Pope

After the papal debacle of Benedict IX, Holy Roman Emperor Henry III was convinced that for the good of the Church he needed to remain involved in the papal election process. Therefore, for the next decade he nominated a series of German bishops for the papacy. Henry believed this process of imperial nomination, election by the Roman clergy, and popular acclamation would solve the issue of meddlesome family and local politics in papal elections. However, he failed to realize that this method relied on the goodness of the emperor and his ability to select virtuous men. What happens when a corrupt king bent on controlling the papacy comes to the throne? It was this concern and a desire to free the papacy from secular control that prompted the proposal of a new method for electing the pope.

Pope Nicholas II (r. 1058–1061) on April 14, 1059, instituted the method of papal election still in use in the Church today: election by the College of Cardinals. Pope Nicholas's *Decree on Papal Elections* was the reformer monk Hildebrand's proposal and stipulated that at the death of a pope, the cardinals were to gather and elect a successor. Placing the election of the pope in the hands of the cardinals was a brilliant move. It elevated the importance of the cardinals and their role in the Church, and it disentangled the papacy from secular control. In future centuries, some secular rulers tried to envelop popes in their sphere of authority, but by that time their main weapon of influence—direct interference in papal elections—had been taken away. In the future, competing national interests infected the College of Cardinals and negatively influenced the election of popes, but Pope Nicholas's decision in the mid-eleventh century was a defining moment in Church history. Now, the papacy was positioned to begin the much-needed internal reform of the Church.

Up Close and Personal:
ST. PETER DAMIAN (1007–1072)

Born in Ravenna near the beginning of the eleventh century, Peter experienced pain and suffering in his early life. His parents died when he was an infant, and he spent the next several years shuffling from sibling to sibling. Initially, a sister cared for him, but then an older and abusive brother and his concubine took Peter into their home, where he was beaten, starved, and sent to work as a swineherd. In the midst of such tribulation, Peter took solace in Christ. While tending pigs one day, Peter found a gold coin in the mud. For a brief moment he thought of all the worldly delights he could buy with his lucky find. However, instead of using the newly found treasure on himself, Peter ran to the parish priest and paid a stipend for the celebration of a Mass for the repose of the soul of his father. Eventually, another brother, named Damian, rescued Peter from his horrible conditions. Damian recognized Peter's intellectual gifts and ensured he received an education in the liberal arts. Peter was so grateful for his brother's love and generosity that he made a lifelong choice. He adopted his brother's name and added it to his own so that, henceforth, he was known as Peter Damian.

Peter was determined to grow closer to God and decided to join the hermitage at Fonte-Avellana. He performed various acts of penance, including immersing himself in cold water until he was numb when tempted by the flesh. In the monastery, Peter believed that developing one's spiritual life was more important than attaining an education. He was not opposed to activities that weren't of a spiritual nature but thought that prayer and other spiritual practices should take precedence. Despite this focus, Peter was no hard-core zealot. He recognized the need for penance, but not to excess. He was not harsh with monks who needed a brief nap during the day. He wrote, "It is indeed better to make a moderate concession to the flesh in sleeping and fervently pray later the praises of God, rather than to spend the whole day sleepily yawning" (quoted in Christopher Rengers, *The 33 Doctors of the Church*, 252). In a radical departure from the religious norms of the day, Peter advocated the reception of Communion daily for his monks as a remedy against the temptations of the flesh.

Besides striving for personal holiness and completing his monastic duties, Peter was a great writer. He produced a biography of St. Romuald (ca. 950–1027), a famous hermit and founder of the Camaldolese order. He was a frequent letter writer and corresponded with every pope during his lifetime, as well as cardinals, bishops, abbots, and laypeople.

Peter's deep love of Mary led to his writings on her role in the economy of salvation and her intercessory powers. He promoted the liturgical custom of keeping Saturday as Mary's day.

Peter realized that Mary leads the faithful to Jesus and his mercy: "My Lord is sweet and my Lady is sweet, because he, my God, is merciful and she, my Lady, is the door of mercy. May she lead us as the mother to the Son, as the daughter to the Father, as the bride to the Groom, who is forever blessed" (Sermon 11). Known as the "Monitor of the Popes," Peter Damian died in 1072. Pope Leo XIII (r. 1878–1903) declared Peter a Doctor of the Church in 1823. His feast day is February 21.

The Reform's Mouthpiece

The history of the Church illustrates that two elements are required for successful comprehensive ecclesial reform: a holy individual clamoring orally or in writing (or both) for reform and a strong pope who makes reform a top priority. The eleventh-century reform movement found its mouthpiece in a saintly man from Ravenna, Peter Damian.

In his late twenties Peter Damian joined a Benedictine monastery. Recognized for his virtuous living and leadership skills, he was named abbot within a decade. Peter's sanctity and virtue drew the attention of Pope Stephen X (r. 1057–1058), and he was created a cardinal in 1057. Later popes sent Peter as legate on special missions to Milan, France, and German territory to settle disputes and convince King Henry IV (r. 1054–1105) to not divorce his wife. Peter was an excellent papal emissary because he sought the favor of no one and did not fear ruffling a few feathers.

Besides his papal missions, Peter devoted himself to reform: first, his own personal reform, then the reform of his monastery, and finally reform of the universal Church. One area of Peter's focus was the immoral behavior of diocesan clergy and monks. Violations against the promise of celibacy, such as keeping mistresses, clerical marriage, and the abhorrent vice of homosexuality, were so widespread by the mid-eleventh century that Peter felt compelled to compose a book on the subject. Addressed to Pope

St. Leo IX (r. 1049–1054), the book, later given the title *The Book of Gomorrah*, expressed Peter's hatred of clerical sexual immorality. The book was not just a diatribe against sin but also an exhortation for personal penance and a return to virtue. Peter wrote in a firm yet compassionate tone. He encouraged priests who were tempted by carnal pleasures to orient "your mind to the grave."[5] In the book, Peter noted that the "cancer of sodomitic impurity" was raging through the clergy "like a cruel beast."[6] Peter did not advocate a witch hunt of the wicked but focused on restoring the virtue of the clergy so the Church could be the light of the world as commanded by Christ. Initially, Pope Leo IX favorably responded to Peter's book and adopted many of his recommendations, but other clerics persuaded the pope that the extent of clerical sinfulness indicated by Peter's work was exaggerated.

Peter also tackled the abuse of simony. In his book *Liber Gratissimus* (Against Simony), Peter argued against the scourge of simony and its evil effects but did not believe that priestly ordinations derived via simony were invalid, a question hotly debated at the time. He also contended that the sacraments performed by simoniac clerics were valid, placing the Church on a path away from a resurgence of the pernicious heresy of the Donatists in the early Church, who argued the validity of the sacraments depended on the worthiness of the minister. Peter's life and writings gave the papal reform movement its spokesman; now it was time for a strong pope to take the stage and enforce the reform.

The Reform Pope

Bruno of Alsace was born into a noble and holy family. His parents, Hugh and Heilewide, were known as pious and learned people. The couple noted young Bruno's aptitude for learning, so his mother endeavored to begin his education. However, Bruno refused to learn from the book she chose to use as his main text. She discovered later the book had been stolen from a monastery and returned it. No longer tainted by the stain of stolen property, Bruno began his studies. The young man commenced a career in the

Church, where his intellectual abilities were soon recognized, along with his personal piety. Eventually, he was consecrated bishop of Toul (in modern-day northeastern France) and remained its ordinary for twenty years until the Holy Roman Emperor Henry III nominated Bruno to become the bishop of Rome.

Those who desired reform in the Church were thrilled with the emperor's choice. Although respectful of the emperor, Bruno made it clear that his election was dependent upon the clergy and people of Rome: "I will go to Rome, and if, on their own accord, its clergy and people choose to elect me for their bishop, I will yield to your desire; but if not, I shall not regard myself as elected."[7] Bruno trekked to Rome, entering the city barefoot and in penitential clothing. He was warmly welcomed by the inhabitants of the Eternal City and was unanimously elected by the clergy and people. Taking the name Leo IX, the new pope focused on three major issues during his pontificate: Church reform, the protection of the Papal States from the Normans, and the resolution of disputes with the Byzantines.[8]

Pope St. Leo IX launched one of the most comprehensive reforms in Church history and did so with great zeal. He began with a synod in Rome in the year 1049, only six weeks after his consecration. The pope condemned the evil vices of simony and violations of clerical celibacy. Notorious prelates guilty of simony were placed on trial, and it is recorded that one, Bishop Kilian of Sutri, dropped dead of a heart attack at Leo's feet while arguing his innocence![9] A year later at another synod in Rome, Leo issued a blanket excommunication of all clerics publicly living in violation of their promise of celibacy.

Leo recognized that authentic reform could not be simply mandated from afar but must be implemented locally, so he traveled throughout Italy, France, and German territories holding synods to enforce reform. Leo was so focused on reform that he spent only six months of his five-and-half-year pontificate in Rome. Wherever he went, the pope deposed immoral bishops and punished clerics engaged in simony, infidelity, and violations of chastity. Leo knew he needed assistance, so he looked to the College of Cardinals. As part of his reform initiatives, he selected men from north of the Alps as cardinals, which was the first time in Church history a pope chose cardinals from outside of Rome.[10] Leo's pontificate was a success in terms of the reform movement. However, his reform initiatives were hampered and his pontificate cut short from the stress caused by a military crisis and a major squabble with Eastern Christians.

YOU BE THE JUDGE:

Were popes chosen by the people?

The method of selecting the pope has differed and developed over the centuries. In the early Church, the clergy of Rome chose the successor of St. Peter from among their numbers. Some records indicate the general populace of the city also played a role.

During the ninth century, powerful Roman aristocratic families vied for the appointment of popes. Elections became farcical as families intrigued, bribed, and battled each other for control of the papacy, which frequently resulted in a less-than-ideal candidate. In the mid-eleventh century, the Holy Roman Emperor Henry III proposed that the emperor would nominate the pope. This method was accepted as a way to remove the influence of rival Italian families, but the imperial nomination required election by the clergy and acclamation by the people before the candidate was recognized as pope. As part of the papal reform movement in the eleventh century, the emperor-nominated method was replaced in 1059 by a new electoral method developed by the monk Hildebrand (the future Pope St. Gregory VII). Hildebrand proposed that the responsibility of electing the pope should be placed in the hands of the cardinals. Pope Nicholas II agreed and issued a decree that stipulated the College of Cardinals would henceforth be charged with electing a new pope. Nicholas's decree also required the assent of the clergy and people of Rome.

Today, the responsibility of electing the Roman pontiff and universal shepherd of the Church rests solely with the College of Cardinals, who are sequestered until the solemn duty is fulfilled.

Chapter 3

The Great Schism and Norman Conquest

The root of the Great Schism between East and West was not theological. It was cultural estrangement, mutual misunderstanding and the hoarded memories of unforgotten feuds.

—*Christopher Dawson*[1]

In the midst of his reform program, Pope St. Leo IX dealt with a vexing group of people from northern France. The Normans were descendants of the Vikings and possessed all the good and bad qualities of their ravaging forebearers. The eleventh century witnessed no greater warriors, conquerors, and general purveyors of mayhem than the Normans. Desiderius of Monte Cassino described these warriors as enjoying "an insatiable enthusiasm for seizing what belongs to others."[2] Norman military skill was renowned throughout the medieval period, and many secular rulers employed them as mercenaries. The Normans also gathered their own forces and launched invasions in order to expand their territory.

Norman military activity in Italy began in the late tenth century when warriors arrived as mercenaries. These men, and later arrivals, realized they could carve out territory for themselves rather than serve Italian and Byzantine masters. Norman military activity in southern Italy alarmed Pope St. Leo IX and numerous Italian secular rulers. The pope, in the midst of his great reform movement, did not want to contend with an additional secular influence that threatened papal independence. As a result, Leo formed a military alliance with secular rulers upset with the presence of the Normans. The papal-led coalition of forces met the Norman army near the town of Civitate in the summer of 1053.

Although the papal armies outnumbered the Normans, the warriors from the North were the premier fighting force at the time, and they won the battle. The Normans captured the pope and held him in captivity for the following nine months. The victory at Civitate solidified Norman military activity in Italy and allowed it to continue. Eventually, one of the Norman commanders at the battle, Robert, nicknamed "Guiscard" or "cunning one," was recognized by Pope Nicholas II as Duke of Apulia and Calabria; he became the future leader of Sicily.

The defeat at Civitate was a blow to Pope Leo personally, but its outcome also affected a more meaningful event. The imprisonment of the pope occurred during a crucial time in the relationship between the Western and Eastern halves of the Church. The pope sent legates to Constantinople to address an issue with the patriarch but was distracted by his incarceration and not able to properly oversee their embassy.[3] This distraction proved disastrous for West-East relations.

The Great Schism

Tension had been building between the two halves of the Church for centuries. In the latter third century, the Roman emperor Diocletian (r. 284–305) administratively divided the empire into halves, beginning the distinction between West and East. That distinction grew during the reign of Constantine (r. 306–337), who moved the imperial capital from Rome to the eastern city Byzantium, which was renamed later Constantinople.

Besides the political changes, the Christian faith in the West and East developed differently theologically as well. Most of the heresies in the early Church erupted in the East as theologians struggled to explain the mysteries of the faith in ways understandable to educated citizens rooted in Greek philosophy and logic. Western bishops largely maintained doctrinal orthodoxy, but the same was not true in the East, especially during the pernicious Arian heresy of the fourth century.

As imperial government changed through the centuries, it influenced Church governance as well. In the West, central governing authority from Rome collapsed in the late fifth century, which led to a more prominent temporal role for the bishop of Rome. In the East, imperial government continued (until the fifteenth century), with the emperors using the Church as their own personal plaything. Eastern emperors dabbled in theology, appointed and discarded bishops, and created a theocratic government wherein imperial civil courts punished ecclesiastic crimes. The emperors used the Church in a relationship known as *caesaro-papism*. This practice resulted in a complete blurring of the lines between secular and religious authority.

As the centuries progressed, the East looked down upon the West and the Roman pontiff as backwater bumpkins, definitely playing second fiddle to New Rome (Constantinople) and its bishop. Eastern bishops were angered by the West's addition of the *filioque* ("and the son") to the Nicene Creed without calling an ecumenical council. This had been done to combat the spread of Arianism, which influenced the West when Germanic barbarian tribes were evangelized by Eastern Arian missionaries. The West was wary of the East, especially because of its frequent embrace of heretical teachings. A violent persecution initiated and maintained by a series of emperors against icons (known as iconoclasm), and those who supported them, began in the East in the eighth century. Later in the ninth century, Photius, a layman made patriarch by an emperor, engaged in a petty schism with Pope Nicholas I the Great (r. 858–867).

In addition to the political, cultural, and theological differences, the liturgical tradition was considerably different in each half of the Church. In the West, for example, Latin was the liturgical language and unleavened bread was used as eucharistic matter, whereas in the East the liturgical language was Greek, the Divine Liturgy was three times as long a ritual as the Western Mass, and leavened bread was consecrated as Eucharist. In fact, the use of leavened versus unleavened bread was a significant theological disagreement between West and East. Some Eastern theologians even argued the use of unleavened bread was invalid matter for the celebration of the Eucharist. Indeed, an Eastern bishop from Bulgaria sent Pope St. Leo

IX a letter in 1053 criticizing him for using unleavened bread: "Straighten yourself out! Correct your errors! Abandon unleavened bread . . . in order to put yourself in accord with us of true orthodoxy!"[4] By the midpoint of the eleventh century, these differences resulted in an infamous schismatic act.

In the year 1024, Eustathios, the patriarch of Constantinople, engaged in a petty dispute with the bishop of Rome. He was jealous that priests pronounced the pope's name when celebrating the Eucharist and insisted Rome allow the proclamation of his name, along with the title "ecumenical patriarch," at every Mass. This title and its use by the bishop of Constantinople had been already previously condemned by Pope St. Gregory I the Great (r. 590–604). Naturally, Rome responded negatively to Eustathios's request. In response, the patriarch blocked the mention of the pope's name at the Eastern Divine Liturgy.[5]

Twenty years later, another patriarch initiated a trivial quarrel with the pope that turned into a squabble of epic proportions affecting the Church for centuries. Michael Cerularius (r. 1043–1058) was "prickly, irascible, and intransigent" and the center of the drama that would engulf the Church in the fateful year of 1054.[6] Possessed of a will of steel, intelligence, and ambition, Cerularius decided to attack the pope and the Western half of the Church. The assault began when the pope's name was stricken from the sacred diptychs (a painting, usually an altarpiece, on two hinged plates that close in the form of a large book) in the imperial capital. This childish action was minor compared to the decision Cerularius made in 1052 to require all churches in Constantinople to follow Eastern liturgical practices, particularly the use of leavened bread for the Eucharist. The imperial capital was home to a large number of Christians from the West who celebrated Mass in accordance with Western traditions. Cerularius's edict, in effect, outlawed the Western Latin-rite celebration of the Mass in Constantinople.

Pope St. Leo IX recognized the patriarch's action required a response. The pope turned to his trusted advisor, Cardinal Humbert of Silva Candida (d. 1061), a man dedicated to the papal reform movement. Humbert possessed a rare skill in the West at the time; he could read and write in Greek. At the pope's request, Humbert wrote a letter to Cerularius protesting his action against Western Christians. The letter, also a pointed defense of papal primacy, was not received well in Constantinople. Pope St. Leo IX knew that letter writing alone would not solve the problem, so he decided to send legates to the imperial city to discuss and resolve the issue with the patriarch.

He chose Frederick of Lorraine, Archbishop Peter of Amalfi, and Cardinal Humbert as papal emissaries. The choice of Humbert was obvious due to his language skills, but usually sensitive diplomatic missions require delicate interpersonal skills such as patience, understanding, and charity. Unfortunately, Humbert was a man of ill temper and quick judgment, and a zealous defender of the pope. Arriving in the imperial capital, Humbert was soon embroiled in a series of pen wars with an Eastern monk named Nicetas Stethatos. The monk wrote a letter criticizing those Christians who use unleavened bread in the Eucharist: "Those who still participate in the feast of the unleavened bread are under the shadow of the law and consume the feast of the Jews, not the spiritual and living food of God. How can you enter into communion with Christ, the living God, while eating the dead unleavened dough of the shadow of the law and not the yeast of the new covenant?"[7] Humbert had no patience with Nicetas and even referred to him as a "pestiferous pimple" and "a disciple of the malignant Muhammad."[8] During their stay in Constantinople, the papal ambassadors were shocked to learn in the summer of 1054 that Pope St. Leo IX had died a few months previously in April. Now that the pope was dead and no successor appointed, the legates lost their authority; their embassy was, technically, at an end.

While they should have quickly departed for Rome, the legates remained in the imperial capital to conduct one final—and disastrous— action. On Saturday morning, July 16, 1054, the legates, led by Cardinal Humbert bedecked in his ceremonial regalia as a prince of the Church, marched into the Cathedral of Hagia Sophia (Holy Wisdom). They processed down the central aisle and, to the astonishment of all, placed a document containing twelve charges against the patriarch and the Eastern half of the Church on the main altar.[9] Along with the twelve accusations, the document excommunicated Michael Cerularius:

> Being unable to bear these unprecedented injuries against
> the chief apostolic see . . . we sign against Michael and his

> supporters the anathema. . . . May Michael the neophyte, who
> improperly bears the title of patriarch . . . and all those who fol-
> low him . . . may they all fall under the anathema, and all the
> heretics, and indeed with the devil and his angels, unless they
> return to their senses. . . . Amen, Amen, Amen![10]

Cardinal Humbert and the other legates had no authority to excommunicate
the patriarch since Pope St. Leo IX had died months previously, and their
action was so offensive to Cerularius that he then issued his own excommunication of the legates and declared the Roman Church heretical. Humbert and his fellow legates packed their bags and quickly returned to Rome.
The cantankerous Cerularius remained in his position as patriarch another
four years until a new emperor, Isaac Comnenus, assumed the throne and
arrested him on trumped-up charges. He demanded an ecclesial trial rather
than resign his office but died in shame before the proceedings commenced.

The actions of Humbert and Cerularius in the summer of 1054 have
been hotly debated through the centuries. Historians question whether the
disagreement actually resulted in a "great schism" or if it was just another
spat in a long line of issues between West and East. The historical record
reflects that Western and Eastern Church officials realized the relationship
was strained, but far from completely broken. In most cases, the political
authorities of the East favored reconciliation, whereas Eastern ecclesial
officials continued to view the West with suspicion and contempt. Patriarch Michael of Anchialus (r. 1169–1177) expressed this view in a letter
to the Byzantine emperor: "Let the Saracen be my lord in outward things
and let not the Italian run with me in the things of the soul, for I do not
become of one mind with the first if I obey him, but if I accept harmony
of faith with the second, I shall have deserted my God."[11]

Despite Eastern Church reticence, a tenuous reunion briefly occurred
in the thirteenth century at the Second Council of Lyons and again at the
Council of Florence in the fifteenth century. In both instances, reunion
was achieved primarily for political and military reasons. At the Council of
Florence, the Eastern delegation actually agreed to papal primacy, but when
news reached the clergy and people of Constantinople, they reacted angrily.

Eastern Church leaders reportedly said, "We would rather see the turban of the Turks over Constantinople than the miter of the Latins."[12] This statement came to fruition fourteen years later when the Ottoman Turks conquered Constantinople in 1453. Sadly, the strained relationship between the Western and Eastern halves of the Church—between Christians who identify themselves as Catholic or Orthodox—continues to the modern day, despite the actions of recent popes to ameliorate the issues dividing the two groups.[13]

Up Close and Personal:
ST. BRUNO OF COLOGNE (CA. 1030–1101)

Bruno was a gifted teacher, administrator, advisor, and religious community founder. Although born in Cologne, Bruno spent much time in Reims, where he completed his education as a youth. Ordained a priest in his native city, Bruno was asked by the bishop of Reims to return to that city to help his former teacher run the schools in the diocese. His successful administration of the education system resulted in his appointment as chancellor of the diocese in 1075.

Consumed with diocesan administration for five years, Bruno could not fulfill his desire to retire from the world in solitude in order to grow closer to God. Circumstances changed and eventually allowed the pious man, along with six companions, to leave Reims and follow a monastic lifestyle. The seven religious settled in the Chartreuse Mountains near the town of Grenoble, where they built a small monastery and founded the Carthusian order in 1084.

Bruno's order was unique in that it combined eremitical (solitary) and cenobite (community) monasticism. The monks lived in separate cells but gathered for communal prayer and fellowship a few times a week. Bruno left the refuge of the monastery in 1090 at the request of his former pupil, Eudes of Châtillon, who had become Pope Urban II. As a member of the papal court, Bruno played an important role in the papal reform movement, especially with the clergy. Bruno wrote commentaries on the scripture, had a deep prayer life, practiced strict spiritual mortifications, and had a great devotion to the Blessed Mother (Ambrose Mougel, "St. Bruno," *The Catholic Encyclopedia*, vol. 3). His feast day is October 6.

Bruno's Carthusians are known for their intense piety and strict obedience to their way of life, prompting Pope Innocent to write that the order "need not be reformed, for it has never been deformed." The Carthusians are famous also for the pale green liqueur known as Chartreuse. The elixir is made from 130 local herbs and flowers gathered by the monks. Carthusians have produced the tasty drink since the eighteenth century from a secret recipe never written down and entrusted to the memory of three monks. When one of the monks dies, a replacement is chosen and entrusted with the formula; the three secret-holders never travel together in order to ensure the survival of the unique spirit.

The Conquest of England

While one contingent of Normans was occupied with conquering territory in southern Europe, the Duke of Normandy had his eye on a prize much closer to home. In the middle eleventh century, the kingship of England was not hereditary but elective. The Witan, an assembly of nobles, chose the king using four criteria: good character, royal blood, English (Anglo-Saxon), and if the previous king had been a reputable man, his heir was closely considered.[14] Usually, these criteria steered wisely the Witan's choice, but in the fateful year of 1066, upon the death of the heirless King Edward the Confessor (r. 1042–1066), the Witan had no fewer than six different possibilities for a successor. They chose Edward's preferred replacement, Harold Godwinson (r. 1066); it was an auspicious choice since it launched a series of decisions and events that shaped English history to the modern day.

England in the mid-eleventh century was not a major political power in Christendom. It was a mostly agrarian society, with little international commerce; its largest town, London, had no more than fifteen thousand inhabitants.[15] The king sat at the top of the political structure along with six earls who controlled large sections of territory (known as earldoms) overseen by multiple thanes, who received rents from the proceeds of villages farmed by serfs. Beneath the earldoms were the shires, which the sheriff, as an agent of the king, administered. Shires were comprised of "hundreds," so called because the land could support a hundred "hides." A hide was the amount of land required to support a family.

Eleventh-century England was at peace, but that was about to change radically. England was not a fortified country because the threat of foreign invasion had stopped once the Vikings ceased their raiding and settled in English lands. Across the channel lay the Normans, a people with entirely diferent aims. Normans were fond of conflict, both internally and externally, and were governed by a powerful duke who was a subject of the French king. In 1035, Duke Robert the Magnificent died and his seven-year-old illegitimate son, William (Guillaume in French), became duke. William's early life was tumultuous as various Norman nobles fought to control him. The constant conflict throughout his life hardened William into a fierce and daring warrior. Indeed, his solid grip on power in Normandy was not achieved until his early thirties. Due to his illegitimate birth, he was known as William the Bastard until the successful invasion of England solidified the epithet he is known by in centuries hence: the Conqueror.

The death of King Edward in England thrust a great opportunity into William's lap. William was a distant cousin of Edward and claimed that the king had promised him the crown in 1051 while he visited England. Additionally, William alleged that Harold Godwinson, on a visit to Normandy in 1064, had told William he could be king upon Edward's death. Now that Harold had accepted the Witan's election, William accused him of being a usurper and oath breaker, and formulated plans to invade England. It is telling that William sought the support of other secular rulers and the pope before launching his invasion of England because it illustrates that his claim to the throne may not have been as secure as he wished. On the advice of trusted theologians and reformers, Pope Alexander II (r. 1061–1073), the first pope elected by the College of Cardinals, blessed William's military campaign. The pope believed William's conquest would contribute to much-needed reform of the Church in England, so he provided the Norman with a papal banner, a ring containing a relic of St. Peter, and excommunicated Harold and his supporters.[16]

Matters became more complicated when another contender, Harald Hardrada, also claimed the kingship of England.[17] Harald was king of Norway and related to Canute (r. 1016–1035), an earlier English king. Harald aligned with Tostig Godwinson, the rebel brother of King Harold, and decided to invade England to make good on his claim to the throne. Harald and Tostig's forces landed in Northumbria and achieved minor victories, including capturing York in September 1066. News of Harald and Tostig's invasion reached King Harold, who was already on the march to engage the invaders. A day after York's surrender, the invaders met the English army at the Battle of Stamford Bridge, where Harald and Tostig were killed and their army routed.

King Harold had no time to enjoy his victory though, as word reached him that William and the Norman army had successfully crossed the channel and landed in southern England. Harold was in a poor tactical position. Nearly three hundred miles north of this new invader, he was forced to march his troops south in order to engage an enemy that had time to secure and expand its beachhead and fortify its position. Eventually, the forces of King Harold and William the Bastard met on October 14, 1066, at Hastings on the southeast coast.

William organized his troops into three divisions and intended to meet Harold's English troops with a battle plan designed to thin his ranks with archers, and engage with infantry and cavalry to exploit holes in the line. The Norman cavalry feigned retreat twice during the battle in order to draw the English into a fatal trap. The fighting was intense, exhausting, and bloody. William was not a rearguard commander. He fought in the thick of battle with his troops and had three horses killed under him. Eustace of Boulogne (the father of the future First Crusade leader Godfrey) replaced one of the horses with his own during the day's engagement. William secured victory when Harold was severely wounded by an arrow to the eye and subsequently hacked to death by a group of Norman fighters that included William and Eustace.[18] William the Bastard had become William the Conqueror. "He had dared—and he had won."[19]

William was crowned king on Christmas Day 1066 and spent the next twenty years consolidating Norman control of the Anglo-Saxon populace, who kept up an active rebellion for years. Normans migrated in large numbers to England and built stone castles to control their conquered lands. Despite his victory and the renown it brought him, William despised the English people and the land. He never learned to speak English (indeed, French was the language of the English royal court for centuries) and lived most of his remaining days in Normandy.

YOU BE THE JUDGE:

Is the filioque *an unauthorized addition to the Creed?*

Words matter. Never has this sentiment been truer than in the centuries-long discussion over the word *filioque*, which means "and the Son." In the fourth century, the Church dealt with the pernicious heresy of the North African priest Arius, who attempted to explain Jesus' relationship to the Father. Roman converts to the faith, many motivated by the recent imperial favoring of the Church, questioned how the Father, Jesus, and the Spirit could all be one God. Arius proposed that only the Father was truly God, and the Son and Spirit were creatures of the Father. The first ecumenical council held at Nicaea in 325 condemned the heresy, but the teaching persisted for centuries. Later in the fourth century, Macedonius and his followers, known as the Pneumatomachi, denied the divinity of the Holy Spirit. A local council in Alexandria and Pope St. Damasus I (r. 366–384) condemned this error, and a statement about the Holy Spirit was added to the Nicene Creed at the second ecumenical council held at Constantinople in 381.

Although the Niceno-Constantinopolitan Creed did not specify the double procession of the Holy Spirit (from the Father *and* the Son), the belief finds expression in the writings of the early Church Fathers. Additionally, Pope St. Leo I the Great (r. 440–461) taught it dogmatically in 447 (see *The Catechism of the Catholic Church*, 247). The addition of the *filioque* to the Creed occurred in the West in the sixth century at the third council of Toledo in 589. This local council added the phrase in order to combat the influence of Arianism among the Visigoth peoples of Spain, who had been evangelized by Arian missionaries. Gradually the addition spread through the West, where a gathering of Carolingian bishops at Aachen in 809 requested the pope officially add the word to the Creed for the universal Church. Pope St. Leo III (r. 795–816) demurred, and it was not until the pontificate of Benedict VIII (r. 1012–1024) that the *filioque* was added to the Creed.

As tensions mounted between the Western and Eastern halves of the Church, especially during the ninth-century Photian Schism, the creedal addition became a serious dispute between Christians. The issue received heightened attention during the mid-eleventh-century series of troubles between West and East that led to the Great Schism. Eventually, though, the Fourth Lateran Council (1215) defined the double procession of the Spirit as a dogma of faith. Eastern Christians officially agreed to this teaching and the word *filioque* at the ecumenical councils of Second Lyons in 1274 and Florence in 1439 when they reunited with the Western Church. Sadly, the union was motivated primarily by Eastern political and military necessities, and was not permanent. Thus, disagreement over the *filioque* continues to the modern day, despite the work of the North American Orthodox–Catholic Consultation, which studied this issue from 1999 to 2003 and promulgated a joint statement on the meaning and use of the contentious word.

Chapter 4

The Investiture Controversy

W hat right have laymen to dispose of ecclesiastical benefices and invest with the crozier
and ring, a ceremony which is the climax
of episcopal consecration?

—*Humbert of Silva Candida*, Against Simony, *1057*[1]

Living in the quiet confines of the monastery, the monk Hildebrand prob-
ably never suspected his life would involve a reign as a Roman pontiff that
changed the Church and the world. Hildebrand was born of lower-class
parents, but an uncle, who was abbot of a strict monastery in Rome, recognized his aptitude. Hildebrand became a Benedictine monk and lived
his days peacefully until he met the reform-minded priest John Gratian,
who became Pope Gregory VI and made Hildebrand his papal chaplain.[2]
Thus began a life of service to the popes that dominated Hildebrand's time
and effort for nearly thirty years.

After the death of Gregory VI, Hildebrand retired to Cluny for a time
until he met Pope St. Leo IX, who brought the monk into his service—and
back to Rome. Hildebrand served the next four pontiffs faithfully, proposing
the idea of papal election by the cardinals to Pope Nicholas II. He was a man
of fiery conviction, deep faith, and passionate focus on reform with a "will of
iron, ceaseless energy, and unshakable determination in adversity."[3] When
Pope Alexander II died in 1073, the cardinals made short work in choosing
his successor in Hildebrand, who did not want the responsibility. He was
more comfortable behind the scenes, advising and directing, without the
limelight and heavy burden. However, Hildebrand reluctantly accepted his
election and chose the papal name Gregory VII. Since he was a deacon at

the time of the election, Hildebrand was ordained first a priest in May 1073 and then a month later consecrated bishop of Rome at the age of fifty-three.

Pope St. Gregory VII (r. 1073–1085) centered his pontificate on rooting out simony, enforcing clerical celibacy, and most importantly, eradicating the lay appointment of bishops.[4] Although the pope recognized the importance of enforcing internal Church discipline, he astutely realized that internal Church reform was fleeting without external independence from secular control. The Church had to be free from the whims of secular rulers in order to fulfill the mandate of Christ to spread the Gospel. Church reform and its universal implementation were central to Gregory's pontifical agenda and were manifested early in his reign when he held a council in Rome in 1074. The meeting produced four reform decrees banning simony, reaffirming clerical celibacy, and providing penalties for violations of both. Gregory sent legates throughout Christendom with the decrees in order to enforce them. Gregory was firmly convinced of his papal authority not only within the Church but also in its extension into the temporal realm. Gregory agreed with the teachings of the late Humbert of Silva Candida (of Great Schism fame) as written in his treatise *Against Simony*. On the relationship between Church and state, Humbert taught the superiority of ecclesial authority:

> The priesthood of the Church is like the soul, the kingdom like the body; they have need of one another. But just as the soul dominates and commands the body, so is the priestly dignity superior to the royal dignity as heaven is to the earth. The priesthood must determine what is to be done . . . kings must follow the churchmen.[5]

For Humbert and Pope Gregory VII, the pope was not just a moral *teacher* but also a moral *judge* with power to absolve or condemn secular rulers with private or even public penances. The ultimate papal weapons in the struggle with secular political power were the spiritual weapons of excommunication and interdict. The penalty of interdict withdrew the celebration of the sacraments from a ruler's domain, placing a heavy burden on the ruler's subjects, which motivated them to advocate for their lord's obedience to papal demands. Excommunication of a secular ruler was even more powerful and disruptive. It freed a ruler's subjects from their moral obligation of support and obedience to the lord and paved the way for legitimate revolution and overthrow of the ruler.

In 1075, a list of twenty-seven decrees, known as the *Dictatus Papae,* was recorded in the papal register. These decrees left no doubt that Pope St. Gregory VII was convinced that his authority was superior to secular rule. Gregory taught in *Dictatus Papae* that the pope alone can depose bishops, the pope is the only man to whom all princes must show obedience, the pope can depose emperors, ecumenical councils cannot be convened without papal approval, the pope cannot be judged by anyone, papal sentences cannot be repealed, and the pope alone can repeal all other sentences.[6]

Up Close and Personal:
MATILDA OF TUSCANY (1046–1115)

Known as "the shield of Pope St. Gregory VII," Countess Matilda of Tuscany was a fierce warrior, leader, and supporter of the papacy in the eleventh century. Educated as a young girl and fond of good books, Matilda showed great aptitude for learning. She married Godfrey the Hunchback of Lower Lorraine, but the couple separated in 1071 and Matilda focused her efforts on ruling her extensive landholdings in central and northern Italy. Her territory was strategic as it encompassed the main road from Italy to German territory through the Alps. Her impregnable castle at Canossa was the scene of one of the most dramatic episodes in the medieval period, when King Henry IV crossed the Alps in the dead of winter to beg forgiveness from Pope St. Gregory VII. Numerous notable works of art depict the scene.

Pope Gregory enjoyed a special friendship with Matilda and her mother Beatrice, referring to them in letters as the "sisters and daughters of St. Peter" (*Regist.*, II, ix). Throughout the Investiture Controversy, Matilda was an ardent supporter of the pope, providing soldiers and money to him when needed. She was known to ride into battle in armor with her troops in the conflict against Henry IV. Matilda bequeathed her lands to the Roman Church in 1077 and again in 1112. Upon her death, a dispute arose between the Church and the German lords over the territory, but eventually Frederick II confirmed the Church's rights to the holdings.

Matilda died of complications from gout in 1115 and was buried in an abbey near Mantua. In the seventeenth century, however, her remains were reinterred in St. Peter's Basilica to honor this great defender of the papacy and faithful daughter of the Church.

Appointing Bishops—Popes or Emperors?

In the early Church, bishops were elected by the clergy and people of the diocese but did not assume episcopal duties until consecrated by other bishops. After the collapse of Western Roman imperial government in the late fifth century, secular rulers began a tradition of appointing bishops. Clovis, the first Christian King of the Franks (r. 481–511), was the first to do so.

Beginning in the ninth century, secular rulers appointed bishops, while the clergy and people of the diocese acclaimed the choice. In German territory, the right of the king to select bishops became a normal aspect of royal functions. Secular rulers wanted control over episcopal appointments because bishops were reliable administrators and the office, along with its temporal landholdings, was not hereditary. As a result, the bishops of the realm tended to side with the king in any conflicts. In the ceremony appointing the bishop, the secular lord gave the appointed bishop a sword or spear; the episcopal ring, the symbol of Christ's love for the Church; and the crozier, a hooked staff that symbolized the bishop's role as shepherd of souls.[7] The new bishop took an oath of fealty to the king and performed an act of homage. Ordination by other bishops, usually the metropolitan, followed this secular ceremony.

Secular appointment of bishops raised the question of whether the Church or the king had authority to choose men for the episcopacy. Additionally, in conflicts between Church and state, the pope could not rely fully on the loyalty of his fellow bishops. This situation was untenable for men focused on reforming the Church and establishing securely its freedom from all forms of secular control. Pope St. Gregory VII now turned his attention to eradicating this practice, but the conflict his opposition created led ultimately to his exile from Rome and death.

The practice of secular investiture of bishops was most prevalent in German areas where King Henry IV (r. 1054–1105) staunchly defended his royal prerogative to appoint bishops. Henry greatly desired the title and crown of Holy Roman Emperor, which his father and grandfather held, but the title was not automatic and required papal coronation. A powerful and stubborn man, Henry IV clashed frequently with the successors of St. Peter. His reign as king (and eventually as emperor) was marked by near constant strife with the Roman pontiffs: three different popes excommunicated him five times. His clash with Pope St. Gregory VII began over the appointment of the archbishop of Milan. The pope and king disagreed on the candidate to assume the archdiocese, and Henry's refusal to relinquish his "right" of appointment led to the pope issuing bans against secular investiture in 1075, in 1078, and again in 1080:

> We decree that no one of the clergy shall receive the investiture
> with a bishopric or abbey or church from the hand of an emperor
> or king or of any lay person, male or female. But if he shall pre-
> sume to do so he shall clearly know that such investiture is bereft
> of apostolic authority, and that he himself shall lie under excom-
> munication until fitting satisfaction shall have been rendered.[8]

News of the pope's ban on investiture reached King Henry, who viewed the edict as an attack on his royal power and ability to govern the kingdom.

Henry used the bishops in his realm for royal administration and as legates of royal authority in dealing with the local barons.[9] The pope knew his decree would anger the king so he sent ambassadors to Henry. The papal emissaries informed the king that any retaliatory behavior on his part would result in excommunication. The king was incensed at the papal message and plotted his next course of action. In the meantime, a brash attack on the pope in Rome further escalated the conflict.

Pope St. Gregory VII was celebrating Christmas Eve Mass in the basilica of St. Mary Major in Rome when armed brigands suddenly stormed into the church and attacked him. Gregory was seized by the raiders, suffering a deep gash on his forehead, and carried to a tower in the city. On Christmas morning, papal forces stormed the tower and released the pope from captivity. Gregory returned to the basilica to complete the liturgy previously interrupted. Afterward, the pope led the traditional Christmas Day procession through the streets of Rome. There was no outward evidence that King Henry was involved in the brazen attack on Pope Gregory, but the event furthered the gulf between the men.

The new year (1076) brought an intensification of the conflict between pope and king over secular investiture of bishops. Henry convened in the city of Worms an emergency meeting of the Diet, a consultative body comprised of German barons and clerics, at which he denounced Pope Gregory as a menace to the peace of Christendom. In a letter to the pope, the king illustrated his anger with the pontiff in the opening sentence: "To Hildebrand, at present not pope but false monk."[10] Henry accused Gregory of simony and forcefully urged him to resign the papacy: "Let another ascend the throne of St. Peter, who shall not practice violence under the cloak of religion, but shall teach the sound doctrine of St. Peter. I Henry, king by the grace of God, do say unto thee, together with all our bishops: Descend, descend, to be damned throughout the ages."[11] Henry encouraged the bishops at the Diet to denounce Pope St. Gregory VII as well, but only one, William of Utrecht, agreed with the royal demand. That bishop's cathedral was soon thereafter struck by lightning. The bishop suffered from excruciating stomach pains a week after the Diet meeting and was dead a month later.

After receiving the king's letter, Pope St. Gregory VII excommunicated Henry IV and absolved his subjects from their obedience and loyalty to him: "I take from King Henry, son of the Emperor Henry, who has risen against the Church with unheard of pride, the government of the entire kingdom of the Germans and of the Italians. And I absolve the Christian people from any oath that they have taken, or shall take, to him. And I forbid anyone to serve him as king."[12] No previous pope had absolved a king's subjects from their loyalty to him. Gregory's letter encouraged open rebellion against Henry, which he hoped would succeed so the Church could be free from the German tyrant, but the king embarked on a wholly unexpected action.

Confession at Canossa

Pope St. Gregory VII's unprecedented act of excommunicating King Henry and absolving his subjects from their fealty to him sparked a political crisis in German territory. The Diet ordered the king to make peace with the pope, or be deposed. The German nobility also requested Pope Gregory's presence at the next Diet scheduled to meet in Augsburg in 1077.

The fifty-five-year-old pope agreed to come and began the journey but stopped to winter over in northern Italy at Canossa, in the territory of his faithful supporter Matilda of Tuscany. Henry, realizing his support among the barons was weak, ventured on a treacherous trip across the Alps in the midst of one of the worst winters in years to make amends with the pope. The king and his small entourage, some of whom lost limbs to frostbite, arrived at the castle in Canossa. The penitential king begged the pope for permission to enter in order to ask forgiveness for his impetuous behavior, but the pope refused. Pope St. Gregory VII left King Henry IV outside the castle gate for three days. Perhaps the pope desired to teach the king a lesson; possibly, he was honestly undecided about what to do. As a priest, he was compelled to reconcile the penitent, but politically his absolution of the king would cause concern for the German nobles. Eventually, the pope relented and allowed the king's entry. Henry begged forgiveness, which Gregory VII accepted, but the pope did not restore the king to his throne: "I restored him to communion only, but did not reinstate him in the royal power from which I had deposed him in a Roman synod. Nor did I order that the allegiance of all who had taken oath to him or should do so in the future, from which I had released them all at that same synod, should be renewed."[13]

Henry IV used his confession at Canossa to reassert his claim to political power. His noble supporters rallied to him, but some German barons, furious at the pope for granting forgiveness to the king, rebelled. The rebel nobles elected a new king, Rudolf of Swabia, who was Henry's brother-in-law, in March 1077. Conflicted on how to resolve the issue of two claimants to the kingship of the Germans, Pope St. Gregory VII balked before finally making a decision three years later (1080) in Rudolf's favor. Furious at the pope's choice, King Henry IV declared the pope a "false monk, ravisher of churches, [and a] necromancer" and appointed an antipope, Guibert the Archbishop of Ravenna, who took the name Clement III.[14] A few months later, Henry's forces killed Rudolf, ending the rebellion.

King Henry IV, secure on his throne and with his antipope in tow, decided to rid himself of the meddlesome Pope St. Gregory VII. German forces marched on Rome, encircled it, and began a three-year-long siege. Eventually, Henry's troops breached the city's defense and captured Rome. Pope St. Gregory VII fled to Castel Sant' Angelo while Henry installed his antipope in St. Peter's Basilica. Then, on March 31, 1084, antipope Clement III crowned Henry IV Holy Roman Emperor. Finally, Henry had secured the imperial crown he most cherished.

Meanwhile, Pope Gregory sought the aid of the Normans in southern Italy in order to regain control of Rome. The Normans gathered troops and began the march to Rome. Hearing news of the Normans' impending arrival, Henry IV withdrew his forces and returned to imperial territory. The Normans arrived at Rome with a large contingent of Muslim troops, who sacked the city for three days, destroying a third of the city by fire.[15] The Roman people were angry with Gregory for inviting the Normans and their foreign troops into the city, so he fled. Traumatized by the recent events, Gregory wrote a letter explaining his actions: "I have been concerned above all that Holy Church . . . should return to her own proper dignity and remain free, chaste and catholic. But because these things were greatly displeasing to the ancient enemy, he armed his members against us to defeat them."[16] Sadly, the pope never returned to his beloved Rome, writing, "I have loved righteousness and have hated iniquity; therefore, I die in exile."[17] He died on May 25, 1085.

YOU BE THE JUDGE:

Did the Catholic Church mandate celibacy in the Middle Ages in order to acquire land and wealth from the clergy?

The myth that the Church mandated celibacy in the Middle Ages is not historically supportable, as the discipline was practiced in the early Church. Although in the first three centuries of Church history there was no law prohibiting the ordination of married men, marriage was never permitted after ordination in either the Western or the Eastern halves of the Church. The Western practice of celibacy for all clergy received papal proclamation in the late fourth century during the pontificate of Pope St. Siricius (r. 384–399), who ruled in February 385 that celibacy was mandatory.

The Church did not mandate the practice of clerical celibacy to acquire land in the Middle Ages because it did not need to do so. The vast majority of Church-owned land was given by faithful men and women as a gift to express their appreciation for prayers answered, as simple business transactions, or from a desire for prayers for their souls.

In the late eleventh century, men sold or gave land to the Church in order to finance their participation in the crusades. One example of this was Stephen of Blois, who was married to the daughter of William the Conqueror and a participant in two crusades. He gave a forest to a monastery before his first journey to the East. In the charter granting the land to the monks, Stephen explained why he donated the land to the Church: "So that God, at the intercession of St. Martin and his monks, might pardon me for whatever I have done wrong and lead me on the journey out of my homeland and bring me back healthy and safe, and watch over my wife and our children." (See Jonathan Riley-Smith, *The First Crusaders, 1095–1131*, 118.)

The Concordat of Worms

Bishop Yves of Chartres formulated a compromise that ended the disruptive Investiture Controversy, which had consumed a king's reign and a pontificate. He argued there were two distinct types of investiture, spiritual and temporal. Religious authority invests spiritually, and temporal authority invests politically.[18] The writings of Yves helped provide the framework for an end to the investiture crisis.

Early in the twelfth century, Pope Callixtus II (r. 1119–1124) and King Henry V (r. 1099–1125) agreed to the Concordat of Worms, a compromise settlement that ended the Investiture Controversy. The king renounced investiture of bishops with the ring and crozier, the symbols of their episcopal office, and the pope allowed the king to invest bishops, before their consecration, with a scepter, the symbol of their temporal office.[19] The concordat was confirmed at the First Lateran Ecumenical Council in 1123, and the rift between Church and state in the German areas ended.

Chapter 5

The Crusading Movement: Part 1

I t is a sign that man loves God, when he casts aside
the world. It is a sure sign that he burns with love
for God and with zeal when for God's sake he
leaves his fatherland, possessions, houses, sons and
wife to go across the sea in the service of Jesus Christ.

—*Eudes of Châteauroux*[1]

In the late tenth century, a mentally unstable man began his reign of
the Fatimid caliphate in Cairo. Al-Hakim initiated a persecution of his
Christian and Jewish subjects, perhaps to illustrate his Muslim bona fides
since his mother was a Christian. He mandated that Christians and Jews,
known as the *dhimma*, wear special clothing and markers in public—ten-
pound copper crosses for Christians and blocks of wood in the shape of a
cow's head for Jews. The mad caliph's persecution continued in the early
eleventh century when he ordered the destruction of one of Christendom's
most revered structures, the Church of the Holy Sepulchre in Jerusalem,
known in the Islamic world as the church of the "dung heap."[2] The church
had been built in the fourth century by Constantine and his holy mother
Helena to enclose the place of Jesus' crucifixion and his tomb. News of its
destruction sent shock waves through Europe, especially in France, where
devotion to the Holy City and the church were high.[3]

This was not the first time Christians and Jews had suffered under
Muslim rule. Violence against indigenous Christians in the East began
with the initial Islamic conquests after the death of Mohammed in the

seventh century. The rout was swift, and by the early eighth century, all ancient Christian territory in the Holy Land and North Africa were under Muslim control. Life for Christians in Muslim-occupied territory was difficult because non-Muslims were viewed as second-class citizens and accorded only restricted rights. A hefty annual tax, known as the *jizya*, which was a form of "protection tax," was required of all Christians and Jews. Although Christians were allowed to keep their faith, there was heavy societal pressure to convert to Islam.

Despite Muslim occupation of the Holy Land, Christian pilgrims from Europe continued to make the trek to Jerusalem. Although always a dangerous journey, Christian pilgrims were allowed freedom of movement (at times) and were generally left alone. However, tensions increased in the eleventh century when troubling news flooded in from the East. Shocking stories—of priests being stoned to death while celebrating Mass in Jerusalem, large groups of pilgrims massacred on Good Friday near the Holy City, Christians forcibly removed from the Church of the Holy Sepulchre (rebuilt in 1049) compound, and the closure of the main pilgrim road—became well known throughout Christendom.[4]

Persecution of indigenous Christians and pilgrims increased dramatically in the late eleventh century with the arrival of a new group of people in the East—the Seljuk Turks. The Seljuks were a nomadic people from the Central Asian steppe who converted to Islam in the tenth century and by the next century controlled the caliphate. The Seljuks invaded the Eastern Roman Empire (also known as the Byzantine Empire[5]) and on August 19, 1071, defeated an imperial army and captured Emperor Romanus IV Diogenes (r. 1068–1071) at the Battle of Manzikert. The Turks continued their march across the imperial province of Anatolia, capturing strategic cities and striking fear into Eastern Christians.

Emperor Alexius I Comnenus (r. 1081–1118) turned to the West for military aid. Alexius sent ambassadors to the pope with a request for help to stem the tide of the Turkish advance. Imperial representatives arrived at the Council of Piacenza in 1095 to ask Bl. Pope Urban II (r. 1088–1099) to send warriors to help them. Urban considered the emperor's request and made plans to call Western warriors to action.

What Were the Crusades?

A crusade was an armed pilgrimage called by the pope whose participants were volunteers who took a vow to complete a penitential journey for promised spiritual benefits (a plenary indulgence). The crusading movement began at the end of the eleventh century and was a just and legitimate response to Muslim aggression against indigenous Christians and pilgrims from Christendom.[6] The movement occupied nearly seven hundred years of Church history and was an integral part of Christian culture and life. Over time, the crusades developed and expanded to include campaigns not only against Muslims in the Holy Land, North Africa, and Spain but also against pagan tribes in the Baltic areas of Europe (modern-day Estonia, Latvia, and Lithuania), enemies of the Church (most famously, Emperor Frederick II), and heretics (especially the Albigensians in southern France). Numerous saints encouraged the faithful to heed papal calls for crusades, and six ecumenical councils legislated and planned for the unique endeavors.

Calling the Crusade

Upon the death of Pope Bl. Victor III (r. 1086–1087), a reluctant pope who desired nothing more than to remain as abbot of Monte Cassino, another man—as strongly committed to the reform and independence of the Church as were his predecessors—was elected pope.[7] Eudes (or Odo) of Lagery came from a knightly noble family and took the papal name Urban II. The new pope immediately pledged to continue the reform policies of St. Gregory VII: "Have confidence in me as you had formerly in Pope Gregory of blessed memory. I mean to follow faithfully in his footsteps; I condemn whatever he condemned; I love what found favor in his sight; I approve all that he considered right and Catholic."[8] Urban followed the policies of Pope St. Leo IX by traveling throughout Christendom in order to implement his reform initiatives. Urban visited France in 1095, the first pope in a generation to do so, and arrived at the town of Clermont, southwest of Cluny, in late November 1095 to attend a local council.

The crusading movement was born at Clermont, on November 27, 1095, as Urban spoke to a large assembly in the open air. Urban's speech was one of the most significant papal utterances in Church history. Despite the significance, there are no direct records of what Urban said that fateful day. However, there are five accounts of the speech all written after the event by authors (Fulcher of Chartres, Robert the Monk, Baldric of Dol, Guibert of Nogent, and William of Malmesbury) who either were present at the council or compiled their version of the speech from those who were. These accounts reveal that Urban's words focused on three themes: the liberation of the Holy City of Jerusalem, the violent activities of the Turks, and an exhortation to Western warriors to take up arms.

The liberation of Jerusalem was paramount to Pope Urban, and he knew it would resonate with the assembled French nobility and knights. There was much devotion in France to the Holy City, and pilgrimages were extremely popular. Jerusalem was considered the center of the world, and its occupation by Muslims was distasteful to the citizens of Christendom. Urban highlighted the importance of Jerusalem in the life of Christ, saying, "This [city] the Redeemer of the human race had made illustrious by His advent, has beautified by residence, has consecrated by suffering, has redeemed by death, has glorified by burial."[9] He pleaded with the French warriors to forgo their selfish desires and goals and come to the aid of Jerusalem: "This royal city . . . is now held captive by His enemies, and is in subjection to those who do not know God. . . . She seeks therefore and desires to be liberated and does not cease to implore you to come to her aid."[10]

Urban's preaching also highlighted the plight of Christians in the Holy Land, who were subjected to cruel tortures and punishments at the hands of the Turks. His graphic description of Turkish atrocities was designed to elicit a visceral response from his hearers so they would readily participate in the armed pilgrimage to liberate their Christian brothers and sisters. Urban reported the various ways the Turks tortured and killed Christians.[11]

Urban appealed also to the warrior ethos of the nobility. Due to his own noble background, Urban was familiar with the mentality of warriors and knew how to motivate knights for the expedition. He appealed to the military adventures of previous great soldiers in French history: "Let the deeds of your ancestors move you and incite your minds to manly achievements. Oh, most valiant soldiers and descendants of invincible ancestors, be not degenerate, but recall the valor of your progenitors."[12]

Finally, Urban offered the spiritual incentive of a plenary indulgence for warriors who participated in the expedition to Jerusalem. Urban decreed, "Whoever goes on the journey to free the church of God in Jerusalem out of devotion alone, and not for the gaining of glory or money, can substitute the journey for all penance for sin."[13] The indulgence formed the very essence of the crusading movement and was the prime motivator for participants.[14]

The response to Urban's call was overwhelmingly positive. When the meeting concluded at Clermont, Urban spent the next year traveling throughout France preaching the crusade. He also commissioned preachers throughout Christendom to urge warriors to take the cross. Some estimates indicate one hundred thousand people may have answered the call, of which sixty thousand were warriors (and six to seven thousand of those were knights).[15] The large response to Urban's call is most impressive when considering the expense of taking the cross. The cost of crusading was significant, requiring four to five times the annual income of a knight.[16] The vast majority of those who took the cross suffered financial hardship as a result of the armed pilgrimage and did not materially profit from it. In order to finance such an expensive undertaking, many knights and their family sold or mortgaged their land and possessions.

Informed of the situation in the Holy Land and urged by the pope to take the cross for the sake of their fellow Christians, the good of the Church, and their own salvation, the warriors and faithful Catholics of Europe began their preparations for the arduous journey east.

Up Close and Personal:

GODFREY DE BOUILLON (1058–1100)

Raised as a knight, Godfrey began his military training at an early age and was a combat-ready warrior by the age of sixteen. Godfrey's family history is replete with fascinating stories and heroic and saintly ancestors. His grandfather, Godfrey the Bearded, was a notorious rebel who fought three times against the Holy Roman Emperor Henry III. Godfrey's great-uncle was Pope Stephen X (r. 1057–1058). His parents were Eustace II of Boulogne and St. Ida of Lorraine.

Crusade preaching was very influential in Godfrey's lands, which enabled him to assemble a vast army. He commanded several thousand knights and soldiers along with two future kings of Jerusalem, his brother Baldwin (the first king of Jerusalem) and his cousin Baldwin Le Bourcq. During the Death March through Anatolia in the First Crusade, Godfrey was seriously wounded while saving an unarmed pilgrim from a bear attack. During the last battle at Antioch, Godfrey illustrated his strength and feat in arms by cleaving an armored Muslim horseman and his mount with one swing of his sword (John C. Anderssohn, *The Ancestry and Life of Godfrey of Bouillon*, 80).

During the siege of Jerusalem in the summer of 1099, Godfrey commanded one of the towers placed along the city wall during the final assault. At one point in the attack, several beams in the tower began to give way and Godfrey stepped into the breach to hold the section together with his bare hands. When the crusaders successfully breached the walls and entered the city in victory, Godfrey took off his armor, put on a simple linen garment, and marched barefoot to the Church of the Holy Sepulchre to pray in thanksgiving for the success of the crusade.

After liberating Jerusalem, the crusade leaders recognized the city needed government, and they asked Godfrey to become king. Tradition holds that the pious warrior rejected the title of king out of deference to the King of Kings. He reputedly remarked, "I will not wear a crown of gold in the city where the Savior wore a crown of thorns." Instead, he took the title "Defender of the Holy Sepulchre." Godfrey defended the kingdom with his life and died only a year later. The heroic and faith-filled Godfrey de Bouillon rightly became the symbol of perfect Christian chivalry for centuries.

The First Crusade (1096–1102)

Urban set the official departure date for the armies of the First Crusade for August 15, 1096, the Feast of the Assumption of the Blessed Mother, and appointed Bishop Adhemar de Monteil, bishop of Puy, as papal legate. The armies planned to travel separately overland and meet in Constantinople.

The main armies of the First Crusade consisted of four groups of French (two), Norman, and German origin. Hugh of Vermandios (1057–1101), the brother of King Philip I, "the Fat," commanded the northern French group, the first to arrive at Constantinople. Count Raymond IV of Toulouse (1041–1105), a fifty-five-year-old veteran of campaigns against Muslims in Spain, which had resulted in the loss of an eyeball, led the southern French group. Raymond was a powerful and wealthy nobleman, who, contrary to the vast majority of armed pilgrims, planned to remain in the Holy Land with his wife, who accompanied him on the journey. Bohemond (1054–1111) commanded the Norman contingent and was, perhaps, the most fascinating crusader. He personally knew Urban II, was fluent in Greek, and was a brilliant military strategist and field commander.[17] Finally, Godfrey de Bouillon (1058–1100), the son of Eustace of Boulogne and the saintly Ida of Lorraine, commanded a large army of German troops. He was "tall, broad-chested, stately, of superhuman strength and courage, [who] was yet chaste, liberal, and a model of Christian piety."[18]

Persecution of Jews

As warriors throughout Christendom prepared to leave on their armed pilgrimage to liberate ancient Christian territory from the yoke of Islam, there were those who, sadly, decided "enemies" nearer to home must be dealt with before journeying to Jerusalem. Jewish communities existed throughout Christendom at the beginning of the crusading movement. Jews were a distinct minority group that often lived separately from the majority Christians. Christian attitudes toward the Jews differed from region to region, but papal policy centered on toleration and protection.

Some warriors, however, used the crusade as an excuse to harass Jews for their wealth; this was especially evident in the Rhineland. Count Emich of Flonheim was particularly grievous in this regard. Emich and his followers marched down the Rhine plundering and massacring hundreds of Jews in the cities of Speyer, Worms, Mainz, Trier, and Cologne. In many cities, the local bishop intervened to protect the Jewish community. Due to this ecclesial interference, Emich changed tactics and took his army to towns without a resident bishop. After leaving a trail of death and destruction in the Rhineland, Emich tried to march through Hungary on his way to Jerusalem. He was denied entry and his army dissolved.

Arrival at the Queen of Cities

The main army groups from Christendom left at different times—before, on, or after Pope Urban's official departure date. The passage through

Europe was mostly uneventful and involved logistical challenges of organizing, moving, and feeding such a large host. Arriving at Constantinople was an eye-opening experience for the crusaders. The imperial capital was a majestic city, much larger than any urban area in Western Europe, and full of churches with thousands of relics.

Although Emperor Alexius had requested military aid from the pope to defend his territory against the Turks, he was shocked at the number of troops that arrived. Western warriors had come to Constantinople in the past to perform military service, but as mercenaries beholden to the emperor for pay and under his command, not as large bodies of independent troops under their own leadership. Alexius was nervous that the crusaders might forget their purpose, turn their military skills against his reign, and capture the city.

A cunning politician whose primary aim was safeguarding his own position and power, Alexius was wary of openly supporting the crusaders in case they failed, which would make relations with the Seljuk Turks on his borders difficult. In order to safeguard his throne, Alexius decided to isolate the crusader leaders and demand their personal loyalty. As the crusaders arrived in the city, the emperor requested they swear an oath to respect his person and return any former imperial lands they liberated. Although there was some initial resistance, the crusade nobles took the oath. After the political maneuverings in Constantinople and a period of rest and refitting, the crusaders were ready to enter enemy territory and begin God's work.

Nicaea, the Death March, and Antioch

The crusaders began their campaign at Nicaea, site of two ecumenical councils in 325 and 787. Nicaea was a strategic city and heavily fortified, but the crusaders were confident of victory. The siege began in May 1097, lasted six weeks, and gave rise to a betrayal on the part of the Byzantines that clouded West-East military relations for the next several crusades. After weeks of heavy fighting, the Western armies prepared their final assault but discovered the imperial banner already flying from the city ramparts. Unbeknownst to the crusaders, Emperor Alexius had opened negotiations with the Turkish garrison to surrender the city. He promised the Turks safety of persons and property and expressly forbade entry of the crusaders into the city. The crusaders believed that the emperor had snatched victory from their hands.

After the siege of Nicaea, the crusade armies began their march through Anatolia to their next objective, the city of Antioch. Life on crusade was extremely difficult and brutal, which is why Pope Urban II counted the journey as a penance worthy of an indulgence. The crusader march through Anatolia was a brutish and nightmarish event. Food and water were scarce as the Turks destroyed sources of sustenance along the route. The toll on men was great, but the toll on horses and other animals was even greater. Most knights arrived at Antioch without any horses at all. Still, the crusaders were involved in a major battle during the march—one that proved their mettle and united their resolve.

Kilij Arslan, the Muslim ruler of Nicaea, had been away during the crusader siege of the city. Desiring revenge for its loss, he pursued the crusade armies and set upon the Christian vanguard forty-five miles southeast of Nicaea at a place known as Dorylaeum. Muslim forces believed they were attacking the main body of crusaders and not just the small vanguard. When the attack commenced, messengers were sent to the main Christian army, three miles away, to hurry to the vanguard's rescue.

In the meantime, Bohemond, as commander of the vanguard, mounted a spirited defense. The main body of Christian troops rushed to the defense of their comrades and successfully stopped the Muslim attack. The Battle of Dorylaeum was a significant crusader victory; it taught the Christians how to fight successfully against Muslim tactics, and as news of the victory spread rapidly throughout Anatolia, it caused panic in the Turkish world.

The crusader army groups continued and arrived at the outskirts of Antioch on October 20, 1097, after a grueling four-month death march through the Anatolian plain. Antioch was an ancient city and had played an important role in early Church history as the home of St. Peter for a time, the place where believers in Jesus were first called "Christians," and the city of the great second-century martyr St. Ignatius. The crusaders assessed the challenge of liberating Antioch. It was a heavily fortified city that rested partly on a mountainside with a defensive citadel perched a thousand feet above the main city. After securing the northern approach to the city, the crusaders marched to the city walls, formed defensive positions around it, and settled in for the siege.

Unfortunately, the crusaders were ill prepared and soon found themselves engaged in a long, drawn-out stalemate of raiding, sallies, and counter-sallies by the Muslims. As the stalemate continued into the winter, the crusaders' sufferings intensified; by Christmas most of the available food near the city was consumed. The knights were forced to kill and eat their mounts, and the rank and file were forced to find and eat small amounts of food even in the most disgusting of places:

> At that time, the famished ate the shoots of beanseeds growing in the fields and many kinds of herbs unseasoned with salt, also thistles, which, being not well cooked because of the deficiency of firewood, pricked the tongues of those eating them; also, horses, asses, and camels, and dogs and rats. The poorer ones ate even the skins of the beasts and seeds of grain found in manure.[19]

Christians were losing the war of attrition outside the gates of Antioch, and they were in the worst possible position: trapped between the walls of the city with the impending arrival of a Muslim relief army. However, Bohemond designed a secret plan to gain entrance into the city. He negotiated with an Armenian convert to Islam named Firuz al Zarrad, who was a captain of one of the tower guards near the St. Paul gate in the northern end of the wall. Bohemond's ability to speak Greek facilitated the exchanges with Firuz, and they discussed the operational details of entering the city. They decided to implement the operation on the night of June 3, 1098. This entailed a commando-type raid in which sixty knights climbed on a ladder to Firuz's tower just before dawn. While the knights reached the tower, as Bohemond's men climbed, the ladder broke. Adapting to the situation, a group of knights in the tower spotted a small, undefended gate near the base of the tower, which they opened, allowing the main body of troops into the city. Once inside, the crusaders were able to fan out through the city, while the remaining Turkish troops retreated to the citadel. The liberation of Antioch, brought about through Bohemond's skilled negotiations, was a miracle and a momentous and happy occasion for the crusaders. Unfortunately, their joy was soon forgotten when a large Muslim relief army arrived outside the gates. One day earlier the crusaders had been the besiegers; now they became the besieged.

The situation looked hopeless until Peter Bartholomew, a layman from Provençal, told the crusade leaders that St. Andrew had appeared to him. The apostle provided the location of the Holy Lance of St. Longinus, the Roman legionary who had pierced the side of Christ on the Cross. Debate raged over the veracity of Peter's vision, but a search was conducted for the relic, and on June 14, 1098, a worn lance head was found in the Church of St. Peter. The discovery of the Holy Lance improved morale, and after spiritual preparation by prayer and fasting, they engaged the Muslim relief army in combat and defeated them outside the gates.

The Liberation of Jerusalem

With the defeat of the relief army, Antioch was securely in crusader hands. After a period of rest and refit, they set their sights once again on their final objective, the Holy City of Jerusalem. The crusaders began the 450-mile march in early 1099 and reached the outskirts of Jerusalem in the summer. Their forces had been greatly depleted over the three years since their departure from Europe; only twelve thousand warriors remained of the sixty thousand who began the campaign.[20]

Once again the crusaders found themselves before the walls of a heavily fortified city lacking proper siege equipment and supplies. As at Antioch, the bleak situation changed with a miraculous vision. This time, a priest named Peter Desiderius told the crusade leaders that he had seen a vision of Bishop Adhemar, the papal legate, who had died almost a year previously at Antioch. Adhemar told Peter that in order to successfully liberate the city, the crusaders needed to fast, pray, and walk around Jerusalem like the Israelites did at Jericho centuries before. Nine days later, on July 15, 1099, after doing as Peter instructed, the crusaders accomplished Pope Urban II's goal: Jerusalem was freed.

Some crusaders went to the Church of the Holy Sepulchre immediately in order to prayerfully thank the Lord for his protection and the success of their mission. Others, however, participated in a rampage of killing and destruction, the tales of which continue to the modern day.[21] The conventions of medieval warfare dictated the offer of surrender terms by a besieging army to a city. Failure to accept terms placed the citizens of a successfully breached city at the mercy of attackers. Although a majority of Jerusalem's population had fled the city before the crusader attack, some inhabitants remained with the Muslim and Jewish defenders and were killed. Christian chroniclers described the carnage in analogies related to scripture passages invoking God's judgment and wrath, but modern observers have misinterpreted these accounts in literal ways not intended by the medieval authors.[22]

Crusader States and Warrior Monks

After the liberation of Jerusalem and the completion of their armed pilgrimage, the vast majority of surviving crusaders left the Holy Land and returned home. They were welcomed as heroes and enjoyed fame in song and memory. Those warriors who remained in the Holy Land realized the need to organize and defend the six-hundred-mile-long newly liberated territory, so they created a kingdom, with counties and a principality. These territories, known to historians as the Crusader States, were the County of Edessa (1098–1144), the Principality of Antioch (1098–1268), the Kingdom of Jerusalem (1099–1291), and the County of Tripoli (1109–1289). Guarding these territories required significant manpower, which the Crusader States never enjoyed. The very nature of the crusading move-ment was episodic, which meant the Christian Latin East was always at the mercy of European participation.

One way the constant manpower shortage was addressed was through the establishment of a radical and unique expression of the religious life: warrior monks. Crusading was a temporary activity, but with the found-ing of the religious military orders, it became a permanent way of life.[23] Two of the main religious military orders were the Knights of the Order of the Hospital of St. John of Jerusalem (the Hospitallers), and the Knights of the Temple (the Templars).

Some of these new orders began as religious institutions with charita-ble missions, but then added a military component because of the needs of the Christians in the Latin East. Bl. Gerard Tenque (1040–1120) founded the Hospitallers in 1113 to serve the sick of Jerusalem. The Hospitallers maintained a large hospital in the Holy City that cared for all patients, regardless of faith, nationality, or sex. The order had a deep devotion to the poor and even referred to themselves as "serfs of the poor of Christ." The military arm of the order garrisoned castles throughout the Crusader States and assisted the kings of Jerusalem and the monarchs of Europe while on crusade. When the Crusader States ended in the thirteenth cen-tury, the Hospitallers settled on the island of Rhodes until displaced by the Ottoman Turks in the sixteenth century. They found refuge on the island of Malta, which they successfully defended against a large Turkish inva-sion fleet in 1565. The order exists today as the Sovereign Military Order of Malta and focuses on its original mission of charity to the poor and sick.

King Baldwin II of Jerusalem (r. 1118–1131) supported a group of knights organized by the Frenchman Hugh of Payns and his companions. The king gave these knights part of his royal palace in the Temple enclo-sure as their quarters. Originally known as the Poor Knights of Christ, the order became identified with the Temple and known as the Templars. The group lived by the Cistercian rule and took vows to live the evangeli-cal counsels of poverty, chastity, and obedience with a special vow to pro-tect Christian pilgrims traveling from the port of Jaffa to Jerusalem. St.

Bernard of Clairvaux (1090–1153) helped recruitment by writing a treatise, *On the Praise of the New Knighthood*, in which he highlighted the meritorious aspect of fighting for Christ with the potential for martyrdom.

The order grew in membership, prominence, and influence in both the Holy Land and Europe. Templar houses were important financial centers and served as places of deposit for Christians traveling to the Holy Land. Those who deposited funds in a Templar house in Europe could withdraw that amount (minus a fee) at Templar houses in the Latin East. As the number of transactions increased, so did the Templar coffers from the surcharges. Their financial holdings and power became the envy of royalty and nobility throughout Europe, but especially in France. This situation exacerbated the jealousy of the despotic Philip IV "the Fair" of France (r. 1285–1314), who arrested the Master of the Order and other knights on false charges. The king convinced Pope Clement V (r. 1305–1314) to suppress the Templars at the Council of Vienne in 1311.

The Second Crusade (1147–1149)

During the First Crusade, a group of crusaders led by Baldwin of Boulogne, the brother of Godfrey de Bouillon, left the main force and arrived in the ancient Christian city of Edessa. An Armenian Christian vassal of the Turks named Thoros was ruler of Edessa. His hold over the city was tenuous as he was unpopular and did not have an heir. Thoros offered to adopt Baldwin as his heir so that the crusaders would help him against the Muslims. Baldwin knew Edessa was a strategic city and readily agreed to the adoption, which proved beneficial. Within a month of his arrival, the populace overthrew and hanged Thoros and recognized Baldwin as their ruler. Baldwin remained Count of Edessa until the death of Godfrey in 1100. He journeyed to Jerusalem to become the first crusader king of Jerusalem. Edessa was the first Crusader State, but its proximity to Muslim-controlled territory and its distance from other Christian areas left it vulnerable to attack. In the mid-twelfth century, the powerful Muslim ruler of Mosul and Aleppo, Imad al-Din Zengi, set his sights on the city.

Zengi desired to increase his power and create an empire by pushing the Christians out of the Latin East. When the Christian ruler of Edessa (Joscelin II) launched an ill-advised military adventure to capture Aleppo in the winter of 1144, Zengi pounced on the then-defenseless Edessa, which he easily captured. Zengi's army rampaged through the fallen city, pillaging, plundering, raping, and massacring six thousand Christian men, women, and children.[24] The first Crusader State, founded almost a half century earlier, was the first to fall back into Muslim hands. News of the city's capture reached Europe, prompting Pope Bl. Eugenius III (r. 1145–1153) to call a new crusade in a bull (*Quantum praedecessores*) addressed to King Louis VII (r. 1137–1180) and the knights of France. Although Pope Eugenius III issued the call for the Second Crusade, it was brought to fruition by the preaching of his onetime tutor, the great St. Bernard of Clairvaux (1090–1153).

The Honey-Sweet Doctor

Bernard was the third son of seven children born to a noble family near Dijon in the Burgundy region of France.[25] The boy was recognized for his brilliance, piety, and handsome features, although his severe ascetic practices left him frail and in ill health for most of his adult life. Bernard had particularly deep reverence, inculcated by his mother, for the Blessed Virgin Mary. In later life, this inspired him to compose the *Memorare* prayer.

In his early twenties, Bernard, along with thirty companions, including four brothers and an uncle, joined the Cistercians, a strict Benedictine reform order. Bernard's holiness and leadership qualities moved St. Stephen Harding, abbot of Cîteaux, to appoint Bernard as abbot of the first Cistercian daughter house at Clairvaux in 1115. Through Bernard's tireless efforts, the Cistercian community grew rapidly.

Bernard was known as an eloquent and effective preacher—one Pope Bl. Eugenius III knew he could rely on to generate a sufficient response for the task at hand. Bernard undertook his papal-directed preaching tour seriously and, despite his ill health, ventured across Christendom for nine months from the spring of 1146 through the following winter.

At the French royal court at Vézaly in front of King Louis VII, Queen Eleanor of Aquitaine, and the French nobility, Bernard's preaching produced so great a multitude of crusade volunteers that the number of prepared cloth crosses, which those who vowed to go on crusade placed on their garments as a sign uniting their journey to the Cross of Christ, ran out. Bernard was forced to tear strips of fabric from his own habit for additional crosses! Bernard's preaching tour also achieved success later that year at the court of Conrad III, king of the Germans (r. 1138–1152), who initially did not want to leave his lands for the crusade. Bernard met with the king privately and persuaded him to take the cross. The next day during Mass, Bernard publicly urged Conrad to go on crusade, and when the king accepted, Bernard took a prepared cloth cross and pinned it on the king's clothes. The dramatic event excited the crowd and led many nobles and warriors to join the expedition.

Conrad's army followed the route of the First Crusade and made its way to Constantinople. Transported to Anatolia, the army began the march to Jerusalem but were annihilated by a Muslim army near the site of the First Crusade's Battle of Dorylaeum. The remnants of the German army continued the march for a time until another battle depleted their ranks and severely wounded the king. The army was forced to retreat to Nicaea while Conrad traveled to Constantinople to convalesce. News of the German defeat reached King Louis VII and his army while encamped at Nicaea. The French army suffered a similar fate on its march through Anatolia. After a disastrous defeat at Mount Cadmus, the army made its way to a Byzantine-controlled port. Despite his pleas, Louis's army was not afforded enough transport ships by the Byzantines to carry the remaining warriors. Instead, only Louis and his nobles were able to embark and make their way to Antioch. The rest of the army tried to travel over land but were massacred.

Louis, Conrad, and their remaining warriors gathered with local Christian nobles in Jerusalem to plan the next course of action in an effort to salvage something from the campaign. The combined Christian army was not sufficient to attack and liberate Edessa, the primary purpose of the crusade, so another plan was devised. The local Christian nobility favored an attack on Damascus because they feared that Nur-ed Din (1118–1174), the son of Zengi, would use the city as a base of operations to harass the Kingdom of Jerusalem. Louis and Conrad agreed; the combined Christian army marched to Damascus and arrived in the summer of 1148. The siege was short lived as the crusaders made a major tactical blunder by abandoning a highly defensible position near the western wall of the city and close to a water supply. Their new position was exposed, their water supply ran low, and then came news that a Muslim relief army was on the way to the city. After four days, the Christian army retreated.

The Second Crusade was a major disaster that negatively affected the crusading movement for a generation. Christians in Europe believed the miraculous success of the First Crusade would accompany all future expeditions. The failure of the Second Crusade cast doubt into the minds and hearts of Christendom. St. Bernard took the news of the crusade's failure personally. He died five years later at the age of sixty-two, leaving a significant impact on both Christendom and the Church.

The Muslim World Unites

Less than thirty years after the end of the calamitous Second Crusade, Christians in the Latin East were terrified to learn that the Muslim world was uniting under the rule of Salah al-Din, which was a title meaning "The Restorer of Religion."[26] Known in history as Saladin, the Kurdish adventurer from Tikrit (in modern-day Iraq) deposed the Fatimid caliph in Cairo and removed the ruling Shi'ites from power. Saladin was not content to be the supreme ruler of the Muslim world; he desired to force Christians from the Latin East. Over the next twelve years, Saladin conducted extensive military raids into Christian territory. He usually withdrew after a short period and in some instances suffered minor military defeats. Saladin remained patient, however, and waited for the perfect time to strike a deathblow to the Kingdom of Jerusalem.

YOU BE THE JUDGE:

Were crusaders motivated by greed and land?

(Note: This section is adapted from my book The Real Story of Catholic History, 97–99.)

One of the most persistent myths about the crusades concerns the motivations of the warriors who participated. A popular false narrative ascribes greed as the primary motive of those who took the cross. The origin of this myth can be traced to the time of the First Crusade and the writings of Anna Comnena, the daughter of the Byzantine Emperor Alexius I. Decades after witnessing the arrival of the crusaders in Constantinople, Anna wrote the *Alexiad*, a book about her father's reign, in which she alleged that noble crusaders came east to get rich while the poor participated to save their souls. Her biased account helped create the misconception that the crusaders were in it for money. This narrative was picked up later by anti-Catholic authors during the Enlightenment who viewed the crusades as enterprises undertaken by the Church to increase its wealth.

The myth that the crusaders were primarily motivated by greed is also based on the "firstborn sons" argument, which stipulates there was a surplus of second-, third-, and fourth-born sons in Europe as a result of a population boom. These sons could not inherit family lands because of primogeniture and, as the false narrative suggests, were constantly warring and disrupting the peace, so the Church decided to marshal these warriors and send them east to conquer land and get rich. The historical record does not support this argument. Medieval people viewed the crusades as a unique opportunity and, as a result, sent their firstborn sons, the most prized progeny, to participate. So, those who went on crusades were usually those who stood the most to lose. (See Riley-Smith, *First Crusaders*.)

Crusaders were also motivated by a love of neighbor. The brothers Geoffrey and Guy participated in the First Crusade and identified helping their fellow Christians as their primary reason for the journey. They wrote they were going "to exterminate wickedness and unrestrained rage of the pagans by which innumerable Christians have already been oppressed, made captive and killed" (*Recueil des chartes de l'abbaye de Cluny*, ed. A. Bruel, v [Paris, 1894], 51–53, no. 3703; *Cartulaire de l'abbaye de Saint-Victor de Marseille*, ed. M. Guérard [Paris, 1857], 1:167–68, no. 143, quoted in Tyerman, *God's War*, 27).

Most people viewed the crusade as a pilgrimage and participated from a deep love for God as well as concern for their own salvation. The warrior class of Christendom believed it was easier for those in religious life to attain salvation. Despite that belief, they desired to offer penance for their sins, and when Pope Urban offered the indulgence to use their weapons for Christ, they willingly volunteered. The pope made it clear that the indulgence was granted only to those who participated "for devotion alone, [and] not to gain honor or money" (quoted in Tyerman, *God's War*, 67). Odo of Burgundy acknowledged this directive when he wrote about his reason for going on crusade: "[I undertook] the journey to Jerusalem as a penance for my sins . . . since divine mercy inspired me that owing to the enormity of my sins I should go to the Sepulchre of Our Savior" (quoted in Giles Constable, "Medieval Charters as a Source for the History of the Crusades," in *The Crusades: The Essential Readings*, ed. Thomas F. Madden, 148).

Lastly, crusading was expensive, and the vast majority of those who survived their expedition returned home poorer for having made the journey. War is costly, and the early crusaders had to personally finance their participation, which often involved selling their land. The motivation to join the armed pilgrimage was hardly ever the potential for material gain; it was the hope of eternal reward.

The Leper King

When Baldwin IV was a young boy, his tutor, William of Tyre, noticed something odd with the child. He did not react to obvious pain stimuli. Diagnosed with leprosy, the young man did not allow his debilitating disease to thwart his studies or duties. Instead, he linked his immense suffering to the sufferings of Christ. In the same year that Saladin became the sole ruler of the Muslim world, Baldwin IV became king of Jerusalem. The sickly king never produced an heir, and his illness required the rule of regents at times, but Baldwin was an outstanding leader and military commander. His mission was to ensure the survival of the kingdom in the midst of dissension, corruption, and the rise of Saladin.

When Baldwin IV died at the young age of twenty-four, his sister, Sybilla, became queen. Sybilla was married to the handsome minor nobleman from Aquitaine, Guy de Lusignan. As queen, she engineered the coronation of Guy as king. It was a calamitous decision that ultimately brought about the end of the kingdom. Guy was an ineffective ruler and bad military commander. His service as regent for a time was so disastrous that the local nobility were openly hostile toward him.

With the death of the heroic Baldwin IV, Saladin knew the kingdom was rife with fear and anxiety and decided the time to attack had come. In late June 1187, Saladin's forces marched into the Kingdom of Jerusalem and made for the city of Tiberias in Galilee. In previous invasions, the Christian strategy had been to wait for Saladin's supply chain to become untenable, forcing his withdrawal. Saladin hoped to avoid that outcome this time by drawing the Christian troops into a decisive battle at a place and time of his choosing.

King Guy decided to march the largest Christian army ever assembled in the kingdom's history to defend Tiberias. Guy misjudged the situation and force-marched his troops in the July heat with no available sources of water. When the Christians arrived at the twin peaks known as the Horns of Hattin on July 3, 1187, they were exhausted and militarily ineffective.

Saladin's troops surrounded the fatigued and thirsty crusaders and, on the morning of July 4, attacked. Although the crusaders fought valiantly, they were in no position (or condition) to achieve victory. King Guy and the relic of the True Cross were captured. All captured Hospitallers and Templars were killed, and many important Christian noblemen were imprisoned.

The defeat at the Horns of Hattin was an earth-shattering event that led to the loss of the Christian cities of Acre, Ascalon, and Jerusalem. In marshaling his grand army, King Guy emptied those cities of their troops in an all-or-nothing attempt to defeat Saladin. He gambled big and lost magnificently. Saladin returned Jerusalem to Muslim control in October 1187. Once in the city, Saladin ordered the removal of every external Christian image and cross and turned most of the churches into mosques. The Holy City of Christ had been in Christian hands for only eighty-eight years.

The Third Crusade (1189–1192)

Christendom was shocked and devastated by news of Jerusalem's fall. Pope Urban III (r. 1185–1187) reputedly died from grief upon hearing the reports. His successor, Gregory VIII (r. 1187), wasted no time calling for a new crusade and promulgated *Audita tremendi*, urging warriors to take the cross and requesting prayers and fasts for the success of the crusade from those who stayed in Europe. Preachers traveled once more throughout Christendom exhorting knights and soldiers—and those in vital support and logistical roles such as carpenters, tanners, and blacksmiths—to liberate Jerusalem. People responded in large numbers, including the three major monarchs of Europe: the king of the Germans and Holy Roman Emperor Frederick Barbarossa (Frederick I; r. 1152–1190), King Richard I the Lionhearted of England (r. 1189–1199), and King Philip II Augustus of France (r. 1180–1223).

The Red-Bearded

Frederick I was a crusade veteran. As a young man in his twenties, he participated in the Second Crusade under the command of his uncle, Conrad III. The experience remained with him, and now in his late sixties, Frederick vowed not to make the same mistakes. The Italians called this man of striking intelligence, vitality, and willpower *Barbarossa*, which means "red beard." Frederick desired absolute power and authority in his domains and, as a result, clashed frequently with the pope. He assembled perhaps the largest army of crusaders ever to leave Europe for the Latin East. It contained most of the leading German nobility, numbered one hundred thousand men, twelve thousand of whom were cavalry; it took three days to pass a single point on the march.[27]

Frederick remembered the issues encountered by previous crusaders with the Byzantines, so he sent envoys ahead of the army to negotiate passage and supplies. Unfortunately, Emperor Isaac II (r. 1185–1195) manifested the Byzantine distrust of Western crusade armies and entered into a secret treaty with Saladin to hamper the progress of the German army.[28] Once inside Byzantine imperial territory, Frederick's army was constantly harassed. Eventually, the Germans were transported to Anatolia, where they met with limited success. They captured the city of Iconium and reached the safety of Christian Armenia. But in June 1190, disaster struck as the aged Barbarossa died while fording the Saleh River. Demoralized by the beloved emperor's death, the remaining troops began the long march home.

The Lionhearted

The third son of King Henry II Plantagenet of England was thirty-two years old when he became king. Known as a brave warrior and accomplished leader in battle, Richard ruled England and half of France. Although king of England for a decade, he spent only six months of his reign in the country and never learned to speak English (like the English monarchs since the Norman Conquest, Richard spoke French). Richard prepared extensively for the crusade by raising money through the "Saladin tithe" and selling his own lands. He decided to travel by sea and raised a large fleet to transport his army to the Holy Land.

The King of France

The twenty-five-year-old son of Louis VII was the complete opposite of Richard the Lionhearted. Although descended from crusading stock, Philip II Augustus was neither a fierce warrior nor an effective leader of men. He was cynical, distrustful, and cautious with an aptitude for self-control and prudence. He could be ruthless but "was usually ruthlessly fair."[29] Philip's reign was marked by incessant political squabbles with the kings of England, who were also his subjects as the lords of Aquitaine. Like Richard, Philip decided to sail his army to the Holy Land.

Philip's French forces arrived in the Latin East at the port city of Acre, besieged since 1189 by King Guy of Jerusalem, who had been released from captivity by Saladin. Guy's army was trapped in a precarious position between the city walls and Saladin's army in the field. The crusaders were not strong enough to take the city and defeat Saladin's relief force until the arrival of the French and then Richard's host in the summer of 1191. After assisting in the liberation of Acre, King Philip, suffering from a malady since his arrival in the Holy Land, decided to leave the crusade and return to France. Those who took the cross were committed for the duration. Leaving before the fulfillment of the crusade vow was frowned upon, and even kings were criticized harshly for such a decision. Philip did not care about the reproach from others and trained his eyes on controlling Richard's land in France.

After the departure of Philip, Richard marched his army along the coast to his next target, the port city of Jaffa near Jerusalem. Saladin's forces shadowed the English army, harassing it with arrows and small skirmishes, biding time and place for a decisive battle. Saladin could not wait for Richard to reach Jaffa, so he ordered an attack in early September 1191 near the town of Arsuf. Richard's military genius won the day, and Arsuf was a Christian victory, although not a decisive one. Saladin, however, would never again risk open battle with the English army.

Over the next few months, Richard pursued military and diplomatic options to bring success to the crusade. Richard captured Jaffa and Ascalon, but he was tiring of the campaign and stalemate. He had left France nearly two years previously and had been actively campaigning in the Holy Land for a year. News of Philip's designs on his French landholdings as well as his younger brother John's plans to take the English throne weighed heavily on his mind. Richard wanted a timely resolution in the Holy Land campaign. Concerned that a victorious siege of Jerusalem was not guaranteed and that the local Christian nobility could not hold the city even if liberated, Richard sought a diplomatic solution.

In early September 1192, Richard and Saladin agreed to a three-year truce, which maintained Muslim control of Jerusalem but allowed Christians free access to the city. Achieving partial success of the crusade objective, Richard departed for home in the fall of 1192. He decided to travel overland on the way home since winter weather in the Mediterranean made sea travel difficult. While traveling near Vienna in late December, he was captured by the forces of Duke Leopold V of Austria, who imprisoned him. Leopold was angry at the actions of Richard's troops during the siege of Acre in 1191, because they threw his standard into the moat so that only Richard's standard remained. Eventually a "king's ransom" was paid and Richard was released. After returning from the crusade and his long imprisonment, Richard reigned for only three more years until his death while besieging the castle of the rebel Viscount of Limoges at Chalus-Chabrol.[30]

Although the Third Crusade was only partially successful, it did shape the future of the crusading movement. Subsequent campaigns followed Richard and Philip's example by traveling to the Holy Land by sea rather than over land. Diplomacy with Muslim rulers was used to achieve some objectives when military force was insufficient to do so.

Chapter 6

The Crusading Movement: Part 2

I f any man will come after me, let him deny himself, and take up his cross, and follow me." To put
it more plainly: "If anyone wishes to follow me to
the crown, let him also follow me into battle, which is
now proposed as a test for all men."

—*Pope Innocent III*, Quia maior, *1213*[1]

When Lothar of Segni was elected pope in early January 1198, he was
the youngest man, thirty-seven years old, chosen as a successor of St.
Peter in a century and a half. He followed the long line of Italian popes
in the twelfth century; only two of the sixteen (Calixtus II, a Frenchman,
and Adrian IV, an Englishman) were from other areas of Christendom.
Lothar came from a noble Roman family and was the nephew of Pope
Clement III (r. 1187–1191), who had created Lothar a cardinal at the age
of twenty-nine. The first university-educated pope, Lothar took the name
Innocent III (r. 1198–1216) and proceeded to have the longest reign in the
thirteenth century.

A Great Medieval Pope

Innocent III was the most influential and significant pope of the medieval
age, but his pontificate is a source of disagreement among historians. Some
portray Innocent III as a megalomaniac who longed to be the lord of the
world and an example of the "evil" influence that the Church can have

in the secular world. Such assessments are oversimplifications. Although Innocent III focused greatly on temporal affairs during his pontificate, this interest stemmed not from a desire to control the world but from a spiritual motivation that oriented him toward the good of the Church. Many modern historians find this difficult to comprehend.[2] Innocent may not have acted correctly in every circumstance, but he did act for the greater glory of God.[3] Navigating the complex and shifting political structures of the time, Innocent believed in the supremacy of papal power even in the temporal world, but he respected the jurisdiction of secular rulers in their sphere of power.[4]

Innocent's pontificate was occupied with the exercise of papal power in both spiritual and temporal realms. Temporally, he focused his authority on limiting the influence of the German emperors who desired to merge their northern Italian lands with their Sicilian territories, which then threatened the independency of the papacy. As an advocate of the supremacy of papal power, Innocent was the first Roman pontiff to systematically use the title "Vicar of Christ," to highlight the authority of the pope.[5] In his inaugural papal address, Innocent described the pope as "higher than man but lower than God."[6] Innocent understood that secular authority was autonomous within its own realm. But he also understood that the pope possessed the fullness of spiritual power, and therefore held that all earthly authority emanated from the authority of the pope. In November 1198, he sent a letter, known as *Sicut Universitatis Conditor*, to the prefect and nobles of Tuscany wherein he wrote, "Just as the moon derives its light from the sun . . . so, too, the royal power derives the splendor of its dignity from the pontifical authority."[7] Contrary to many modern misinterpretations of the man and his ministry, Innocent had no desire to rule the world. He did, however, expect kings to assist him in the work of evangelization, in the defense of Christendom, in the reliberation of Jerusalem, and in the maintenance of a just Christian society for the faithful.

The crusading movement occupied a significant portion of Innocent's papal agenda. He yearned for the recovery of Christian territory in the Holy Land, and in an attempt to achieve that goal, he called more crusades than any other pope. Innocent referred to the crusading movement as the business of the cross (*negotium crucis*) or sometimes the business of the crucified (*negotium crucifixi*).[8] In his 1213 bull *Quia maior*, Innocent announced that taking the cross was a moral imperative for Christian men: "To those men who refuse to take part . . . we firmly state on behalf of the apostle Peter that they . . . will have to answer to us on this matter in the presence of the Dreadful Judge on the Last Day of Severe Judgment."[9]

Innocent envisioned the crusades as managed and administered by the Church and introduced several innovations to the crusading movement designed to further participation in the armed pilgrimages. In order to help finance the costly expeditions, he taxed the clergy and instituted the placement of "crusade boxes" at the back of parish churches for the faithful to deposit money. In order to encourage wider participation, Innocent expanded the spiritual benefits granted to crusaders. He offered a plenary indulgence not only to those who fought in person but also to those who paid for a proxy to fight in their stead, for the proxies themselves, and for those who provided material aid to crusaders.

The Fourth Crusade (1201–1205)

In the first year of his pontificate and six years after the end of the Third Crusade, Innocent III called his first armed pilgrimage. The pope knew participation might suffer while Richard the Lionhearted and Philip II warred against each other, so he focused his efforts on bringing peace to their kingdoms. His peace endeavors were successful, but when Richard was killed besieging the castle of a rebel subject in 1199, Innocent's crusade seemed in doubt.

A knightly tournament in France revived the effort. Count Thibaut III of Champagne (1179–1201) was a powerful and wealthy nobleman with important political connections. Thibaut came from crusading stock; his grandparents were King Louis VII, who led the Second Crusade, and Eleanor of Aquitaine, who went along on the journey. Thibaut's father, Count Henry I, fought in the Second Crusade, and his brother, Henry

II of Champagne, reigned as king of Jerusalem (r. 1192–1197) after the death of King Guy.

Upon hearing the news of Innocent's crusade, Thibaut decided to take the cross in keeping with family tradition. He decided to make his public crusade vow profession at a large tournament he hosted on Sunday, November 28, 1199. His witness motivated other knights at the tournament to take the cross, including Geoffrey of Villehardouin, an over-fifty veteran of the Third Crusade who was captured at the siege of Acre and spent four years in a Muslim prison. Innocent's crusade now had the manpower it needed to embark on the campaign.

The French barons assembled early in 1200 to discuss logistical and operational plans for the upcoming crusade. They decided to follow the travel plans of the Third Crusade and sail to the Holy Land, but no one had ships, so a delegation of six men were sent to Italy to find transport. The barons knew that Venice, Genoa, and Pisa sent two fleets a year to the Latin East, but since Genoa and Pisa were at war, the delegation traveled to Venice. The barons met with the aged Enrico Dandolo (1107–1205), the ruler (known as the "doge") of Venice, who was in his nineties and blind. The French barons negotiated a treaty with Dandolo that required the Venetians to provide transport and personnel to support 4,500 horses, 4,500 knights, 9,000 squires, and 20,000 infantry for a combined force of 33,500 men at a cost of 85,000 marks of Cologne. Venice agreed to ready the fleet by the end of June 1202. The agreement was unprecedented and involved the cessation of Venice's merchant activity for a year![10]

Although the envoys were successful in arranging passage for the crusade host, the Treaty of Venice contained a serious flaw that haunted the expedition and resulted in one of the most infamous episodes in the crusades. The treaty was flawed because the ambassadors based the calculation of payment on a future unknown number of potential recruits and not on the known number of warriors at the time of negotiations. This was risky since crusaders not subject to lords who were going to Venice were not required to take the Venetian transports. If less than the agreed number of warriors arrived in Venice, the crusaders would not have enough money to pay the Venetians.

In the summer of 1202, crusaders began to assemble in Venice at the appointed time for departure. Unfortunately, the flaw in the treaty became a serious problem when only 13,000 of the expected 33,500 crusaders arrived. As a result, the crusaders could not pay the bill, and the Venetians were faced with a financial crisis of epic proportions. As the summer drew to a close, the Venetian doge, Dandolo, developed a plan to remedy the situation. Dandolo suggested that the crusaders capture the city of Zara, a town on the Dalmatian coast 165 miles southeast of Venice. The booty from the conquest would compensate the Venetians for the cost of building the crusader fleet. Zara had once been Venetian territory but rebelled and was now under the control of King Emeric of Hungary (r. 1196–1204). The city was important to Venice because it was the first port along the Adriatic coast and had been used for refurbishment and resupply of ships traveling to the Latin East.[11]

Although the doge's plan solved the financial quandary, it produced a moral one. King Emeric had taken the cross in 1200, and as a crusader, he received Church protection of his lands; attacking them would bring excommunication. The warriors wanted to pursue their objective but could not afford their transport. They were obligated to fulfill the stipulations of the treaty, but they risked their souls in attacking a fellow crusader's land. Serious debate erupted in the crusader camp, and when the decision was made to accept Dandolo's plan, some troops left for home, but the majority prepared for the attack.

When news of the plan to attack Zara reached Pope Innocent, he furiously dispatched letters to the crusade leaders forbidding them to assault Zara on pain of excommunication. The noblemen hid these letters from the rank and file in order to proceed with the attack. The Venetian fleet arrived at Zara in November 1202, and the crusaders prepared for battle. Incredulous that fellow Christians would attack their city, the inhabitants draped cloth crosses over the ramparts to remind the crusaders whom they were fighting. The ingenious tactic did not work, however, and the

Zarans sued for peace. After the city surrendered, the French sent envoys to Pope Innocent asking forgiveness for their participation in the attack. The pope granted their request and lifted the excommunication on the condition they restore Zara to the king of Hungary and promise to not attack other Christian lands unless there was just cause and only after receiving papal approval.

The Venetians did not follow the French example as Dandolo did not believe they had done anything immoral. The Venetians remained excommunicated for the remainder of the crusade. It was clear the crusade had been highjacked by the Venetians, but Innocent remained committed to the liberation of Jerusalem and believed the expedition could continue on its path. The arrival of envoys from a renegade Byzantine prince, however, soon proved otherwise.

Up Close and Personal:
JEAN DE JOINVILLE (1225–1317)

Jean de Joinville was born in 1225. Jean was educated in the military arts, learned to read and write, and studied Latin. As a young man, Jean made the famous pilgrimage to the shrine of St. James at Compostela in Spain. When the First Crusade of King Louis IX was announced, Jean took the cross. He came from a crusading family; his grandfather fought and died in the Third Crusade; two uncles participated in the Fourth Crusade, and his father fought in the Albigensian and Fifth Crusades. Jean made his spiritual preparation for the crusade by walking barefoot as a penitent touring local shrines before his departure. Jean and ten companions landed at Cyprus to join the main French army. Initially, Jean did not place himself in the service of King Louis but planned to finance his own journey by mortgaging his lands. He ran out of funds, however, while on Cyprus. Desperate, he reached out to the king and entered into royal service upon which the king subsidized his participation in the crusade. Jean fought bravely during the Egyptian campaign and was wounded during the action at Mansourah, where Robert, the king's brother, died. Taken into captivity by the Muslims along with the king, Jean remained imprisoned until the king's ransom. Twenty years later when the king decided to venture forth on crusade again, Jean tried to change the king's mind but was unsuccessful. This time Jean did not journey with his king on crusade. Early in the fourteenth century, Queen Jeanne de Navarre, wife of King Philip IV the Fair, the grandson of Louis IX, asked Jean to write a book about the saintly king. The eighty-year-old Jean complied with the queen's request and dedicated the book to her son, Louis, who became king of France in 1314. Jean's *Life of Saint Louis* recounts details of the king's life and his first crusade. It was the first work about a saint's life written by a layman, and since Jean was a close friend and advisor to the king, the work provides an intimate portrait of one of the most important personages of the medieval period.

Trouble in Constantinople

Byzantine imperial politics were cold, calculating, and savage. When Alexius III (r. 1195–1203) overthrew his older brother, he blinded the deposed ruler and shoved him in jail. In the fall of 1201, Alexius Angelus, the son of the imprisoned emperor, fled the court of his uncle and arrived in the West. While the crusaders rested and resupplied during the winter at Zara, Alexius sent envoys to the leaders with an offer. He wanted the crusaders to take him to Constantinople and restore his father to the throne. In return, Alexius promised to unite the Eastern Church with Rome, join the crusade to Jerusalem with an army of ten thousand soldiers, garrison at his expense a troop of five hundred men in the Holy Land, and pay the crusaders two hundred thousand silver marks, which was enough to clear their debts and finance the rest of the expedition.

When news of the renegade Byzantine prince's offer reached Pope Innocent, he reacted quickly by sending a letter to the crusade nobles instructing them to ignore Alexius. Innocent warned the crusaders against traveling to Constantinople and "not to return to their previous sins (attacking another Christian city) like dogs returning to their own vomit."[12] Unfortunately, the crusade leaders ignored the pope's warning and offered to help Alexius, summoning him to Zara. The decision to assist Alexius was extremely unpopular with the army, which believed the leadership was ignoring the liberation of Jerusalem, the primary objective of the crusade. Many warriors left the army rather than attack another Christian city. Those who stayed hoped the diversion to Constantinople would prove short. The upstart prince arrived in Zara during the spring of 1203, and preparations commenced for the voyage to Constantinople.

Arriving in the summer of 1203, the crusaders were awestruck at the ancient jewel of a city, the likes of which had no equal in the West. The ten largest cities of Western Europe could easily fit within the walls of Constantinople, a cosmopolitan city containing large minority populations of westerners, Jews, and Muslims. The city's defensive fortifications were impressive and consisted of three and a half miles of huge triple walls staggered in height and thickness with towers, as well as a wide and deep moat that surrounded the outer wall. The city had not fallen to a besieging army in its nine-hundred-year history.

Alexius Angelus had convinced the crusaders that the citizens of Constantinople would welcome their arrival. They were dumbfounded when confronted by a threatening messenger from Alexius III. The visit seemed to indicate that the citizens did not know the crusader army included the deposed emperor's son. So, Dandolo devised a plan to sail Alexius Angelus in a galley along the city walls. At times, the galley came within ten feet of the walls and the crusaders called out to the inhabitants to recognize their returning lord. Instead of cheers and excitement, the flotilla was met with jeers, curses, and objects thrown in anger. Dismayed at the response, the crusaders realized they faced the daunting task of attacking the city despite the small size of their force. Villehardouin, who later wrote a detailed account of the crusade, succinctly described the situation: "Never have so many been besieged by so few."[13]

The assault on Constantinople's walls began in July 1203 with separate attacks by the French and Venetian forces. The French attack did not succeed, but the Venetians captured several towers and a section of the wall. Their position was not secure, and when Byzantine reinforcements arrived, the Venetians withdrew. In their retreat, the Venetians set a defense fire to separate their force from the Byzantines, but the fire raged out of control and burned a significant portion of the city. Although the crusader attack was defeated, Alexius III squandered an opportunity for a decisive victory. His failure brought severe criticism, and recognizing his life was at risk, Alexius III decided to flee the city in the middle of the night.

The departure of Alexius III provided an opportunity for the crusaders. The people did not want Alexius Angelus as emperor because he was associated with the Western army responsible for attacking the city. Instead, Isaac II, the deposed and imprisoned emperor, was released and restored to the throne. Newly reinstalled, the emperor requested the presence of his son, and after receiving assurances from Isaac that the stipulations agreed to by Alexius Angelus would be honored, the crusaders allowed the prince to enter the city. A few weeks later, Alexius Angelus was crowned co-emperor, taking the name Alexius IV. The crusaders were allowed into the city and spent time visiting the numerous churches and sacred relics.

Meanwhile, Alexius IV began fulfilling his promises to the crusaders. Alexius IV and patriarch John X Camaterus sent a joint letter of obedience to Pope Innocent III. The co-emperor paid half (one hundred thousand silver marks) the money owed, but the crusader nobles soon clamored for the remainder. In order to accumulate the remaining funds, Alexius IV taxed wealthy families and then ordered the tombs of past emperors opened in order to confiscate the precious vestments and jewels on their corpses. When even that proved insufficient, Alexius IV shockingly embarked on sacrilege by seizing icons and sacred vessels for their precious metals and jewels. Not surprisingly, Alexius IV's actions deeply angered the people and clergy of Constantinople.

Eventually, in late January 1204, the imperial bureaucrat Alexius Ducas, nicknamed *Mourtzouphlus*, or "thick brows" (because of the large bushy eyebrows that met in the middle of his forehead), staged a coup with the backing of the military, clergy, and imperial civil service. Alexius IV was imprisoned, and the aged co-emperor Isaac II died soon afterward. Mourtzouphlus was crowned emperor, taking the name Alexius V. He tried unsuccessfully to remove the crusaders and came to believe that they would leave if Alexius IV was dead, so he ordered the young man's strangulation. The crusade nobles were furious to learn about the death of Alexius IV because the Byzantines still owed the crusaders money. The murder of Alexius IV was answered by another crusader siege of the Queen of Cities.

The second siege of Constantinople commenced in April 1204 and resulted in one of the most notorious events in history. The crusaders succeeded in gaining entry into the city, which caused panic and a general retreat of the imperial guard, and the flight of Alexius V. The crusaders then proceeded to engage in the customary three-day sack of conquered cities. The suffering endured by the citizens of Constantinople was significant; some were killed, abused, and raped. However, there was no wholesale massacre or slaughter as was also customary at the time in cities after a successful siege. The crusaders removed enormous amounts of wealth, including sacred items and relics, which were shipped to the West and placed in the churches and cathedrals of France and Venice.

When Pope Innocent III received news of the sack of Constantinople, he was shocked, saddened, and angered by the actions of the crusaders. The crusade was an unmitigated disaster despite the pope's frequent attempts to steer it toward its holy objective. The nobles had ignored him and chosen to follow the upstart Byzantine prince's path to perdition. Innocent wrote them a scathing letter:

> You rashly violated the purity of your vows; and turning your arms not against the Saracens but against Christians, you applied yourselves not to the recovery of Jerusalem, but to seize Constantinople, preferring earthly to heavenly riches. . . . These "soldiers of Christ" who should have turned their swords against the infidel have steeped them in Christian blood. . . . They stripped the altars of silver, violated the sanctuaries, robbed icons and crosses and relics. . . . The Latins have given example only of perversity and works of darkness. No wonder the Greeks call them dogs![14]

Of all the crusades that spanned the centuries, the Fourth Crusade is the most well remembered. It remains a source of tension between Christians in the East and the West and is frequently cited as a prime example of the evils of the crusades. Although many parties were responsible for the disaster of the Fourth Crusade and the sack of Constantinople, it is clear that Pope Innocent tried to prevent the sack. Absent the invitation of Alexius Angelus, the Western warriors would not have traveled to the city in the first place.[15]

The Fourth Lateran Council

Pope Innocent III learned many lessons from the fiasco of the Fourth Crusade; chief among them was the need for the Church to administer and control future military exploits in the East, which he tried to accomplish with the Fifth Crusade. Besides the crusade, Innocent called for a new ecumenical council in his April 1213 bull *Vineam Domini*. He summoned the Church's bishops to gather in Rome in the fall of 1215 to discuss reform efforts as well as plans for the new crusade.

The twelfth ecumenical council was a spectacular event and a crowning achievement of Innocent's pontificate. Over four hundred bishops, eight hundred abbots, the Latin patriarchs of Constantinople and

Jerusalem, thousands of clerics, and even the religious founders Francis and Dominic attended the gathering.[16] The council produced seventy decrees encompassing topics such as the Eucharist, using the word *transubstantiation* to explain how bread, wine, and water become the Body, Blood, soul, and divinity of Christ. The council condemned the Albigensian heresy raging in southern France and instructed bishops to investigate reports of heresy in their diocese. The council established the so-called Easter Duty, a requirement of every Catholic (over age fifteen for men, and age twelve for women) to confess their sins and receive Holy Communion at least once a year, preferably during the Easter season.

Innocent III promulgated plans for the Fifth Crusade, developed at the council, in the decree *Ad liberandam*. Crusaders were to assemble at Messina (Sicily) and Brindisi (on the Adriatic coast of Italy) on June 1, 1217, with the goal of liberating Jerusalem through an attack on Egypt. The Church attempted to control and administer the Fifth Crusade from the beginning, but as the old military axiom stipulates, no plan survives first contact with the enemy.

The Fifth Crusade (1218–1221)

Pope Innocent III died in 1216 as preparations for the Fifth Crusade were underway. The cardinals elected Cencio Savelli, who took the name Honorius III (r. 1216–1227) as his successor. Nearly two years after Innocent's death, the warriors of the Fifth Crusade landed in Egypt. Their first objective was to capture the town of Damietta, which was two miles inland from the mouth of the main branch of the Nile River. The town was on the most direct approach to Cairo, the capture of which was necessary to support an invasion of the Holy Land and a march to Jerusalem.

Although Pope Innocent III envisioned strong ecclesial leaders directing the crusade, it still required the presence and actions of competent military men. Sadly, the Fifth Crusade suffered from a lack of both. Frederick II, king of the Germans, took the cross and repeatedly promised to go to Egypt but never arrived with his much-needed army. Two papal legates, Cardinal Robert from England and Cardinal Pelagius from Portugal, were chosen to oversee the crusade, but Cardinal Robert died early in the campaign. Cardinal Pelagius was a severe and brazen man who did not engender confidence and engaged in questionable decision-making throughout the campaign. Pelagius exercised control over the crusade because of his position. As treasurer, Pelagius maintained and distributed the campaign's money, which allowed him to exert his own will, much to the detriment of the endeavor.

While besieging Damietta, a Muslim army attempted to remove the crusaders by a surprise attack. The crusaders successfully defeated the Muslim attack, which prompted Egyptian sultan al-Kamil to offer a diplomatic solution. In return for the crusader withdrawal from Egypt, the sultan offered a thirty-year truce and, except for a few strategic castles, the return of the previous territory of the Kingdom of Jerusalem conquered by Saladin. The crusade nobles encouraged Pelagius to accept the generous offer, but the cardinal rejected it. Pelagius believed the crusaders were in a position of strength and had no need to negotiate.

As the siege of Damietta slogged on into the summer of 1219, the crusaders witnessed the arrival of a strange group. Francis of Assisi and twelve companions arrived at the crusader camp with a desire to convert al-Kamil to the faith and end the crusade. (See the next chapter's You Be the Judge feature on page 115.) Although their mission of evangelization was unsuccessful, the presence of Francis and his brothers provided a welcome distraction from the drudgery of the siege.

The siege ended nearly six months after the Franciscan visit, when some crusaders noticed a defensive tower was unmanned and entered the city. As the soldiers entered Damietta they were met with a horrific sight: dead bodies everywhere. The year-and-a-half siege had reduced food availability to starvation levels and led to the deaths of tens of thousands. The preacher and chronicler Oliver of Paderborn described the ghastly scene and smell that greeted the crusaders: "As we were entering [Damietta], there met us an intolerable odor, a wretched sight. The dead killed the living."[17]

When al-Kamil heard the news of Damietta's capture, he once more offered a diplomatic solution. Cardinal Pelagius rejected it again, believing still that the crusaders were in a superior military position. The crusaders remained in Damietta for a time awaiting reinforcements. In the summer of 1221, however, they decided to march halfway to Cairo to the city of Mansourah. The army arrived near the city but chose to encamp in a precarious defensive position. Muslim troops took advantage of the situation and cut the crusaders' supply line. Faced with the untenable situation of advancing on Mansourah without adequate supplies or digging fortifications and waiting on additional troops, the crusaders realized the only acceptable military solution was a tactical withdrawal back to Damietta. The crusaders were harassed by Muslim attacks as they retreated, but eventually the army returned to the city.

Since Frederick II had failed to arrive with additional troops and the advance on Cairo was stalled, Cardinal Pelagius finally realized it was time for diplomacy. Peace terms with al-Kamil were reached in the summer of 1221 and involved an eight-year truce and the crusader withdrawal from Egypt. The Fifth Crusade was launched with great hope and was on the cusp of great success, but like previous crusades, it ended in failure.

The "Crusade" of Frederick II (1228–1229)

One of the most colorful and scandalous figures of the Middle Ages was Frederick Hohenstaufen (1194–1250), the son of Holy Roman Emperor Henry VI (d. 1197) and Constance of Sicily (d. 1198). The grandson of Frederick Barbarossa, little Frederick was well educated and spoke six languages—including Arabic—fluently. Upon his mother's death, Frederick became king of Sicily, which proved politically problematic for Pope Innocent III. If Frederick was anointed Holy Roman Emperor, papal territory would be surrounded by imperial territory in northern Italy and by the Kingdom of Sicily in the south. Frederick promised Innocent III that he would abdicate the Sicilian throne when anointed emperor, but he did not honor that promise. Political troubles between Frederick and the popes dominated the early thirteenth century and resulted in several excommunications and a crusade against the impious king/emperor.

Frederick was a medieval outlier. He was very individualistic, religiously skeptical, and pragmatic, with great affinity for Islam, all of which earned him the nickname *stupor mundi* (wonder of the world). A contemporary chronicler noted, "Of faith in God he had none. He was a crafty man, wily, avaricious, lustful, malicious, and wrathful."[18] Frederick had an appreciation for Islam that was not only extremely rare but also a cause of scandal in medieval society. He had a Muslim bodyguard and a harem stocked with Muslim women.

Despite his tolerance for Islam, Frederick took the cross in 1215 to participate in the Fifth Crusade but never left for Egypt. Six years later he renewed his vow and promised his former tutor now turned pope (Honorius III) that he would depart for the Holy Land in late June 1225. When the time came to venture on crusade, Frederick made excuses and asked the pope for an extension. Honorius III granted the request but told Frederick he had to leave on August 15, 1227 (twelve years after his first vow). Frederick was fully aware that failure to meet these promises carried the penalty of excommunication.

In the spring of 1227 Pope Honorius III died. The cardinals elected Ugolino Conti, a fifty-seven-year-old canon lawyer, scripture scholar, and diplomat, who took the name Gregory IX (r. 1227–1241). Gregory IX was the grandnephew of Innocent III and, like him, a proponent of the crusading movement. When Frederick II stalled in his crusade preparations, Gregory IX did not have the patience of his predecessor. Gregory demanded Frederick fulfill his vow in a letter to the tardy king.

Frederick complied and prepared for the journey to the Latin East. His troops assembled in Brindisi in the summer of 1227, but the squalid conditions of the camp combined with the summer heat produced a disease that ravaged the army. Many soldiers died, and desertion became a problem as men fled from the illness. When the emperor arrived, he found a debilitated and dismayed force but prepared to depart regardless. The fleet sailed on the Nativity of the Blessed Virgin Mary, September 8, 1227, but Frederick became ill at sea and canceled the expedition. Illness, however, was not an acceptable reason for failure to fulfill the crusade vow, and Frederick's return prompted Pope Gregory IX to issue the threatened excommunication.

The following year, Frederick ignored the fact that excommunicated persons were forbidden to participate in crusades and prepared once more to travel to the Holy Land. Gregory IX warned the emperor not to go to the Holy Land and advised the Christians in the Latin East against dealing with the renegade ruler. Frederick arrived in September 1228 and immediately opened negotiations with al-Kamil. A few months later, in February 1229, Frederick and al-Kamil agreed to a treaty, which allowed Christian control of the cities of Jerusalem, except for the Temple area, Bethlehem, and Nazareth, for ten years. Frederick also promised military assistance to al-Kamil if attacked by Christian forces. The emperor's unofficial crusade had reaped significant dividends.

The following month, Frederick entered Jerusalem in order to claim the throne of the kingdom, which was rightfully his infant son's, Conrad.[19] Frederick decided to enter the Church of the Holy Sepulchre in a brazen act of self-coronation. Because the emperor had been excommunicated, there was no ecclesial representation at his coronation. The recalcitrant emperor did not stay long in Jerusalem, leaving two days after his spectacle in the Holy Sepulchre. He journeyed to Acre, where he stayed for several months, until leaving for home in May 1229. He tried to leave clandestinely in the early morning hours but had to pass through the butcher's quarter en route to the docks, where he was pelted with tripe and entrails.[20]

Despite the irregularities of Frederick's "crusade," the "wonder of the world" accomplished a great deal for the Christians in the Latin East. Although Frederick's venture was diplomatically successful, his political situation at home was precarious. Frederick tried to consolidate his power as both king of Sicily and Holy Roman Emperor and fought politically and militarily in a power struggle against several popes. The situation between emperor and pope reached critical mass in early 1240 when Frederick invaded the Papal States. Because of Frederick's invasion and incessant attacks on the papacy, Gregory IX proclaimed a crusade against the tyrant. The conflict with the emperor negatively affected the health of Pope Gregory IX, who died in the summer of 1241. After the brief reign of Pope Celestine IV (1241) and an interregnum of eighteen months, Pope Innocent IV (r. 1243–1254) was elected to the papacy and proved a staunch opponent of Frederick.

YOU BE THE JUDGE:

Did Pope St. John Paul II apologize for the Fourth Crusade?

(Note: This section is adapted from my book The Glory of the Crusades, 159–61)

The sack of Constantinople by Western warriors in the early thirteenth century has tainted East-West relations ever since. Some historians have contributed negatively to this difficult and complex relationship by their descriptions of the event. Sir Steven Runciman (1903–2000), for example, believed "there was never a greater crime against humanity than the Fourth Crusade" (Steven Runciman, *A History of the Crusades*, vol. 3, 130).

The sack was devastating in terms of the amount of wealth and relics purloined by the Western warriors, but to write that it was a great crime against humanity only six years after the end of the Holocaust was the epitome of exaggeration. It is true, however, that the sack remains one of the enduring memories of the crusades. Most people recall the event, or at least the false narratives about the event. Because of this, it continues to be used to further the falsehood that the crusades were primarily land-grabs or military exploits motivated by greed and desire for booty.

The Fourth Crusade was plagued by a series of bad decisions, overzealous calculations, and the need to fulfill treaty obligations. Crusade leaders veered off course, ignored repeated admonitions from Pope Innocent III, and pursued a course of action that led to the sack of Constantinople. Despite numerous papal protestations at the time, blame is still placed inappropriately with the Church for the events of the Fourth Crusade. When Pope John Paul II visited Athens in 2001, he was greeted by Greek Orthodox monks protesting his visit holding signs with "1204" (the year of the sack) printed on them.

Modern-day critics of the crusades mistakenly believe Pope St. John Paul II apologized for the Fourth Crusade and the sack of Constantinople. In brief remarks during the visit of Ecumenical Patriarch Bartholomew I to Rome on June 29, 2004, eight hundred years after the Fourth Crusade, the pope described the events of the spring of 1204 and recalled the prohibitions of Pope Innocent III against the crusade's diversion to Constantinople:

> On this occasion we cannot forget what happened during the month of April 1204. An army that had set out to recover the Holy Land for Christendom marched on Constantinople, took it and sacked it, pouring out the blood of our own brothers and sisters in the faith. Eight centuries later, how can we fail to share the same indignation and sorrow that Pope Innocent III expressed as soon as he heard the news of what had happened? (John Paul II, "Welcome Address to the Ecumenical Patriarch Bartholomew I," June 29, 2004, 3).

The saintly pontiff recognized the complexity of historical events and the inherent problems associated with interpreting them from a modern worldview. He said, "After so much time has elapsed, we can analyze the events of that time with greater objectivity, yet with an awareness of how difficult it is to investigate the whole truth of history." Urging the reconciliation of the two halves of the Church, St. John Paul II offered a prayer: "Let us pray together, therefore, that the Lord of history will purify our memory of all prejudice and resentment and obtain for us that we may advance in freedom on the path to unity."

The First Council of Lyons and the Death of the Emperor

The crowning achievement of Innocent IV's eleven-year pontificate was the First Council of Lyons in 1245. Nearly two hundred bishops from across Christendom gathered to discuss clerical immorality, the spread of heresy, the capture and destruction of Jerusalem in 1244 by the Muslims, the continuing schism of the Byzantines, and the persecution of the Church by Frederick II.[21] The council convicted Frederick of sacrilege and heresy and deposed him. The battle between pope and emperor, a major skirmish in a long conflict between Church and state in the West, ended on December 13, 1250, when the "crusader without faith" died.[22]

Within five years of the expiration of the treaty between Frederick and al-Kamil, Jerusalem was controlled once more by a Muslim ruler bent on eradicating the presence of Christians in the Holy Land. The Egyptian ruler as-Salih Ayyub wanted to restore his great-uncle Saladin's empire. To that end, he hired a mercenary army of Khwarazmians, a Muslim people driven from their lands in the 1220s by the Mongols. The fierce Khwarazmians captured Jerusalem in the summer of 1244, killed a large number of Christians, and desecrated the sacred places. News of the killings and loss of the Holy City prompted the calling of yet another crusade and the leadership of a saintly king.

King St. Louis IX (1214–1270)

The king was deathly ill; indeed, one attendant believed at one point that he had died. But when Louis, king of France, heard about the suffering of Christians in the Latin East and the Muslim capture of Jerusalem, he acted and took the cross on his sickbed. The king's mother tried talking the pious king out of such an adventure. Unsuccessful, she managed to persuade the archbishop of Paris to declare that a vow taken while sick was not binding. Louis was determined to go on crusade, so when he recovered, he took the cross again. King Louis IX (r. 1226–1270) stood much to lose by going on crusade. He was king of the wealthiest and most populous country in Christendom, but his love for Christ and the Church outweighed any and all temporal concerns.

Louis was born on April 25, 1214, at Poissy and was the second son of Louis VIII (r. 1223–1226) and Blanche of Castile (1188–1252). The future king's father fought in the Albigensian Crusade in southern France, which brought that area under royal control, so that his son was the first monarch of France to rule over both parts. Louis VIII died in 1226 at the relatively young age of thirty-eight, when Louis IX was only twelve years old. A child king had not ruled in France in over a century and a half, and the young Louis was not even a knight. That deficiency was rectified on his way to Reims for his coronation. Since Louis was not of mature age, his mother ruled as regent until 1235 when Louis turned twenty-one. Louis married Marguerite de Provence in 1234. Their marriage was happy but suffered from the interference of the Queen Mother:

> The unkindness that the queen Blanche showed to the queen Margaret was such that she would not suffer, in so far as she could help it, that her son should be in his wife's company, except at night when he went to sleep with her. The palace where the king and his queen liked most to dwell was at Pontoise, because there the king's chamber was above and the queen's chamber below, and they had so arranged matters between them that they could converse in a turning staircase that went

from one chamber to the other; and they had further arranged
that when the ushers saw the queen Blanche coming to her son's
chamber, they struck the door with their rods, and the king
would come running into his chamber so that his mother might
find him there; and the ushers of Queen Margaret's chamber
did the same when Queen Blanche went thither, so that she
might find Queen Margaret there.[23]

Louis and Margaret's marriage union produced eleven children (six
boys and five girls). Several of the children died young; three were born
during his first crusade and three after his return.[24] Louis's offspring
ensured that he became the ancestor of all subsequent kings of France, a
fact recalled centuries later by the priest on the scaffold with Louis XVI
in 1793 when he called the condemned monarch "a son of St. Louis."[25]

Like many in Christendom, Louis IX was a deeply pious and devout
Catholic, but even in an age of faith, the king's personal piety and sanctity stood out. He was concerned for his own salvation but even more so
for the salvation of his subjects. He enjoyed the preaching of the mendicants (Dominicans and Franciscans), read theological works, especially
the writings of St. Augustine, and studied scripture. His personal piety
was expressed by simple clothing and a devoted prayer life. Louis awoke
each night at midnight to participate with his royal chaplains in the Liturgy of the Hours and offered fifty Hail Marys each evening, kneeling and
standing for each prayer.[26] Louis went to sacramental confession weekly
and maintained both a daytime and a nighttime confessor in order to
receive the sacrament when needed.[27] In keeping with the practices of
medieval piety, the king received Communion infrequently. In his case,
he received the Eucharist six times per year on the feasts of Easter, Pentecost, the Assumption of Mary, All Saints, Christmas, and the Purifica-
tion of Mary.[28]

Louis's prayer life was amplified by penitential practices including
fasting; wearing a hair shirt, a common penitential practice; and a special habit described by William of Saint-Pathus: "The saint king abstained

from laughing as much as he could on Fridays, and, if sometimes he started to laugh unexpectedly, he would stop himself immediately."[29] Louis greatly enjoyed life and joking so the mortification of not laughing one day a week was a serious and difficult penance. Like most medieval Christians, Louis was very interested in relics and pursued their acquisition in order to venerate the sacred objects. His most famous acquisition was the Crown of Thorns, redeemed from the Venetians who had acquired it from Baldwin II, the Latin emperor of Constantinople in 1237. The procurement of such a holy relic moved Louis to build a special chapel, the Sainte Chapelle, in Paris to house it.

Louis was known as a dutiful father who loved his children and considered it his greatest duty to teach them the Catholic faith, especially through personal example. Although sometimes separated from his children due to the requirements of the realm, Louis wrote letters to them in which he passed on his fatherly and saintly advice. In a letter to his son Philip, Louis instructed him to remember that God should hold primacy of place in one's life and to "fix your whole heart upon God."[30] The king also warned his son to stay free from the stain of mortal sin, which kills the soul and threatens one's salvation. Louis instructed Philip to "resolve not to commit mortal sin, no matter what may happen and you should permit all your limbs to be hewn off, and suffer every manner of torment, rather than fall knowingly into mortal sin!" Louis exhorted Philip to frequent the sacrament of Confession and encouraged his son to remain devoted to the pope and to support and defend the Church.

The First Crusade of Louis IX (1248–1254)

Eighteen years into his reign, Louis decided to embark on his first crusade. Louis personally managed the preparations for the crusade and heavily subsidized his fellow crusaders. Crusading for Louis was a family affair. On his two crusade expeditions his brothers, their wives, and even his own queen accompanied him. The army, comprising mostly French but also groups of Norwegians, Germans, Italians, and Englishmen, left the manmade port of Aigues Mortes on August 25, 1248. The fleet sailed for Cyprus to spend the winter, rest, and prepare for the expedition.

Louis decided on a campaign that mimicked the Fifth Crusade. Sadly, it did so in almost every respect, including the end result. His force arrived at Damietta in June 1249, where the king led an amphibious assault. The opposing Muslim force retreated to the sultan's camp and away from the city, and Louis took Damietta easily. Louis convened a council of war to determine the next course of action. He made the decision to march on Cairo, and most of the army departed Damietta in November 1249. Robert, the king's brother, and a vanguard of French knights were killed when they advanced into Mansourah without the support of the main force. After the failed attack on Mansourah, the army lacked the strength to press on to Cairo. Still, Louis did not want to retreat to Damietta, so they held their ground. The Muslims realized the crusader army was in dire straits so they attacked frequently and moved to cut off the Christians' supply lines. Disease and starvation overtook the crusader camp, and the Muslims captured supply convoys from Damietta.

After two months, Louis realized a combat retreat was necessary so he ordered a withdrawal, but it was too late. Surrounded and taking heavy casualties, the king knew the campaign was over, so he sought terms with the Muslims. The new sultan, Turan Shah, ordered the execution of the sick and wounded and imprisoned the nobility, including King Louis. Turan Shah knew that a siege to recapture Damietta from the crusaders would be a costly affair, so he negotiated a deal with Louis. The sultan agreed to release Louis in return for a crusader withdrawal from Damietta and the payment of a huge sum of money; the payment of half would release Louis from prison. Louis agreed, and Queen Marguerite worked tirelessly to collect the ransom. When half the amount was collected, Louis was released in May 1250.

Surveying the failed campaign in Egypt, the remaining French nobles urged Louis to end the crusade and return home. Louis allowed any knight who wanted to return home to do so, but he decided to stay and travel to the Holy Land. He remained in the Latin East for the next four years, building up the defenses of the Christian coastal cities. In 1253, news reached the king that his beloved mother Blanche had died, and after an absence of six years, Louis knew it was time to return home. The experience of crusade radically changed Louis: the pious king before became the penitential and saintly king afterward. He increased his penitential practices and continued to dream of the liberation of Jerusalem.

The Second Crusade of Louis IX (1269–1272)

In the fall of 1260, the Mamluk general Baybars installed himself as sultan in Egypt. Baybars was a fierce, blue-eyed Russian Turk (Kipchak) with a gift for soldiering and administration and a desire to reestablish Saladin's empire. Baybars began a campaign of *jihad* to eradicate the Christians from the Holy Land using a scorched-earth policy. He ordered the destruction of all captured Christian areas and massacred and enslaved the populace.

Baybars's campaign was swift and deadly, and the future of the Kingdom of Jerusalem was in serious doubt. Urgent appeals were sent to Europe for another major crusade, while Baybars sacked Jaffa (1268) and captured the previously impregnable fortress of Krak des Chevaliers (1271), a Hospitaller stronghold that not even Saladin had captured. Panic reached an apex after Baybars sacked the city of Antioch. His troops killed every Christian in the city, including all women and children, making it the single greatest massacre in crusading history. Christians would never control the city again. The scourge of Baybars the merciless demanded a response, so once more the saintly crusader-king of France took up the cross.

Louis took the crusade vow for the second time on March 25, 1267, along with his brothers, three sons, and most of the great nobles of France. Louis was older now, a man in his fifties, and it had been twenty years since he had first left on crusade. In the summer of 1270, the French army once more left Aigues Mortes on their holy journey. The crusader fleet sailed to Tunis, the choice of which is something of a mystery. Louis's decision to travel there may have been motivated by reports that the emir of the region was willing to convert to the Faith. Or the decision may have been prompted to support his brother, Charles I, the king of Naples and Sicily, and rid the area of an opposing ruler. Perhaps logistics were the reason for the choice. Every crusader fleet from Europe needed a muster port and a place to winter over. On Louis's first crusade, the fleet had stopped for the winter on Cyprus. Tunis was closer and easier to reach than Cyprus.

Regardless of the rationale, the French fleet arrived in July. Louis's army landed and moved inland to Carthage where they awaited reinforcements. The summer heat was intolerable, and health conditions in the camp quickly deteriorated. In early August, Louis's twenty-year-old son Jean Tristan, born at Damietta during his first crusade, died. Sickness ravaged the camp, and by the end of the month, the king himself was deathly ill. Sick and bedridden for a month, King Louis IX finally succumbed to his illness. He died at 3:00 p.m. on August 25, 1270, while mouthing the words, "Jerusalem, Jerusalem."[31]

Louis IX was the last monarch of Christendom to go on crusade. The crusading movement continued, but it would never witness campaigns as well financed and prepared as those of Louis IX. Nevertheless, despite the royal interest, organization, and manpower, the crusades of Louis IX were abject failures, and the Crusader States ended twenty years later with the fall of the city of Acre in 1291. The Church recognized the piety of the French king almost thirty years after his death when Pope Boniface VIII (r. 1294–1303) canonized St. Louis IX, the last monarch of the Middle Ages so recognized.

Chapter 7

Crisis in England and the Beggar Monks

St. Francis and St. Dominic came from God and returned to Him, passing through the world like twin meteors. . . . They became conscious of their mission at virtually the same moment. . . . Dominic had only fifteen years to work, Francis twenty. In those two decades they transformed Christendom leaving their mark upon it forever.

—*Warren H. Carroll*[1]

Thomas Becket came from a Norman family that immigrated to England after the Conquest by William.[2] Becket was sent to school in Paris and eventually became a clerk for Theobald, the archbishop of Canterbury. Theobald noticed Becket's intellect and virtue and ordained him a deacon in 1154. When the young Henry Plantagenet became king (Henry II, r. 1154–1189) in the same year, he chose Becket as his chancellor.

Despite their difference in age (Becket was twelve years senior), the two men became close friends. Becket was handsome, tall, witty, a great storyteller, and fun company. Henry was very much the opposite of his older friend. The king had a sharp temper, was not as handsome as Becket, and as one contemporary wrote, "he had an enormous paunch, rather by the fault of nature than from gross feeding. He waged a continual war, so to speak, with his own belly by taking immoderate exercise."[3]

Henry relied on his close friend for important missions, including military expeditions where Becket engaged in combat despite his diaconal ordination. His personal piety was renowned as he eschewed foul language and acts of immorality. Theobald died in 1161, and King Henry spent the next year planning the appointment of Becket to the esteemed post of archbishop of Canterbury. Becket had no desire to be named archbishop and made his thoughts known to the king, but Henry dismissed his concerns. Henry appointed his friend to the prestigious post, and the pope accepted the appointment. Because he was only a deacon, Becket was first ordained a priest and then the following day ordained a bishop.

A great change occurred in Becket upon assuming the ancient see of St. Augustine of Canterbury, the famous missionary sent to England by Pope St. Gregory the Great in the sixth century. He devoted his time to the poor, to ascetical spiritual practices like the wearing of a hair shirt, and to other penances. Becket's growing dedication to the Faith was not what Henry expected.

Henry had believed that with his close friend as archbishop, he would easily control the Church in his realm. The king was displeased with how ecclesial courts handled crimes committed by clerics. Since the beginning of Henry's reign, English clerics had committed a large number of murders and the king believed they were receiving lenient sentences, because canon law did not allow ecclesial courts to impose the death penalty. The king wanted secular courts to have jurisdiction over clerics accused of secular crimes. Henry believed Becket would accede to his wishes, but the archbishop steadfastly rejected the royal demand. Henry was stunned and disappointed with Becket's reaction and continued to press his friend to acquiesce. When the king demanded Becket's obedience to his royal authority in November 1163, the archbishop responded:

> You know how loyal I have been to you, from whom I expect only a temporal reward. How much more ought we to do faithful and honest service to Almighty God. . . . You are indeed my lord, but He is my lord and yours. It would be useful neither to you nor to me if I were to neglect His will in order to obey yours. For on His fearful Day of Judgment you and I will both be judged as servants of one Lord.[4]

Emboldened by Becket's tireless defense of the Church, the bishops of England stood firm against the encroachment of the king on their authority. The crisis continued into the new year of 1164 when, at an assembly of bishops and barons at Clarendon, the king demanded from Becket a public apology and capitulation to his demands. The archbishop refused once again, so the king ordered the English bishops to agree to sixteen propositions known as the Constitutions of Clarendon.

The constitutions revealed that the king was not interested merely in punishing wayward clerics but sought the complete control of the Church. The most egregious of Henry's demands included the following: jurisdiction of royal courts over clerics accused of secular crimes, clergy could not leave England without the king's consent, no royal official or vassal could be excommunicated or his lands placed under interdict without the king's permission, no appeal to the pope from decisions rendered in royal courts without the king's permission, and revenue from vacant dioceses would go to the king until election of a new bishop with the king's assent. Becket refused to agree to the king's outrageous demands.

Furious, the king began to persecute his friend over the next several months, in a heavy-handed attempt to get Becket to change his mind. Becket was convicted of false charges, levied with hefty fines for alleged wrongdoing as chancellor, and declared a traitor to the Crown. Eventually, Becket fled England to escape the king's wrath. He sought shelter in France and brought his case before Pope Alexander III (r. 1159–1181). The pope supported Becket and implored Henry to cease his persecution against the Church.

While in exile, Becket publicly called for Henry to revoke the Constitutions of Clarendon or risk excommunication. The king refused and instead seized all Cistercian monasteries in England because the order had provided refuge to Becket in France. A delicate game of diplomacy and letters followed among king, pope, and archbishop. The pope urged Henry to restore Becket to his see in 1169, and when that request went unheeded, he wrote another letter in 1170 reiterating the demand and threatening England with interdict, a punishment that forbade the celebration of sacraments in an area if the king failed to comply. Eventually,

Becket believed it was time to return to England, which he did in November 1170. A month later, the king, while campaigning with his army in Normandy, and perhaps influenced by a night of partying and drinking, indicated his displeasure with Becket to a group of knights. The angry king said, "What disloyal cowards do I have in my court, that no one will free me of this lowborn priest!"[5]

Four knights—William de Tracy, Hugh de Morville, Richard Brito, and Richard FitzUrse—took the king's words as an imperative and left France bound with royal vengeance for Becket. They returned to England and approached Becket on December 29 in his cathedral. They clamored, "Where is the traitor?" and "Where is the archbishop?"[6] Finding Becket, a rage-filled knight said, "Now you will die, for we cannot let you live any longer!"[7] The archbishop responded, "I am ready to die for my God, and for defending the justice and liberties of the Church. But if you seek my life, in the name of Almighty God and under pain of excommunication, I forbid you to hurt anyone else who is here—either monk, priest, or layman, but let them be as safe from the penalty as they have been innocent of the crime."[8] As one knight raised his sword to cut down the archbishop, Becket cried out, "I commend myself and my church to God and the Blessed Virgin Mary, to St. Denis, and St. Alphege."[9] Edward Grim, a monk from Cambridge, who before that day had never been to Canterbury or met the archbishop, had his arm cut off when he raised it to try to defend Becket. A knight struck Becket in the head, and the archbishop muttered, "Into thy hands, O Lord, I commend my spirit; for the name of Jesus and the defense of the Church, I embrace death."[10] The knights unleashed a violent spasm of sword thrusts and hit Becket in the head several times, which spilled his brains on the floor of the cathedral. One knight cut the archbishop's head off with a force so violent that the blade broke in two when it hit the pavement. When news reached Pope Alexander, he was so horrified and angered by the killing that he refused the mention of Henry's name in his presence for a week.[11]

The king was greatly troubled by the death of his onetime close friend. Henry made a public atonement for the death of Thomas Becket during his act of penance in 1174. The king processed barefoot and in penitential clothing to Canterbury cathedral where he kissed the site of Becket's killing, provided funds for candles to burn continuously in memory of the archbishop, and was publicly whipped by several bishops, an abbot, and eighty monks.

After their murderous deed, the four knights also felt remorse and endeavored to make amends. A year after their sin, the knights traveled to Rome and begged forgiveness from Pope Alexander III. The pope heard their Confession, absolved them of their sins, and gave them the crusade as a penance. The warriors joined the Templars and made their way to the Latin East, where they eventually died protecting Christians and defending the Holy Land.

The life and death of Archbishop Thomas Becket illustrates the conflict between Church and state in the medieval period. The relationship was always tumultuous; at times, it was a healthy tension. Becket refused to accede to the whims of the monarch, and like Pope St. Gregory VII before him and Pope Boniface VIII after him, the valiant cleric suffered much for the independence of the Church.

Up Close and Personal:

ST. ANTHONY OF PADUA
(1195–1231)

Except for St. Francis himself, St. Anthony of Padua is the most well-known Franciscan in Church history. Born in Lisbon, Portugal, to noble and pious parents, he was baptized with the name Ferdinand. At the young age of fifteen, Ferdinand joined the Canons Regular of St. Augustine in Lisbon but moved after two years to Coimbra (126 miles north of Lisbon) to a more secluded place away from friends and relatives so he could focus on prayer and study.

It was at Coimbra in 1220 that Ferdinand became aware of the Friars Minor, when the bodies of the first Franciscan martyrs from an evangelization mission to Morocco were brought to the church. Inflamed with a desire to witness for Christ to the point of martyrdom among the Muslims, Ferdinand left the Canons and joined the Friars Minor, taking the religious name Anthony. Attempting to follow in the footsteps of the Franciscan martyrs, Anthony set out for Morocco, but a severe illness prevented him from accomplishing his task.

Anthony desired anonymity in order to focus on his spiritual life, but an event at Forli (south of Bologna) changed his life and reputation. Present at an ordination of Franciscan and Dominican friars, Anthony was chosen unexpectedly to preach when it was discovered no other religious was prepared to do so. Anthony preached extemporaneously with such deep knowledge and insight on the scripture that the assembled friars were completely astonished. When St. Francis was informed of Anthony's preaching, he directed the friar to teach theology to his brothers.

Anthony drew large crowds when he preached due to his eloquence and booming voice. He dazzled crowds with his knowledge, memory, and exhortation to virtue. Anthony also preached against heresy, and no heretic could defeat the pious friar in debate.

There are many tales of wonders and miracles attributed to Anthony. A horse reportedly refused to eat until he adored the Blessed Sacrament brought before him by Anthony. And heretics allegedly offered him poisoned food, which he rendered inert with a blessing. Anthony, like Francis, loved God's creatures and famously preached to the fish from the bank of the Brenta River near Padua (Italy). There is also an account of Anthony bilocating: during a sermon he realized he was supposed to be in choir with the friars, so he appeared at the same moment in choir and in the church in order to accomplish both tasks. The infant Jesus appeared to Anthony, and the miraculous apparition forms the common artistic representation of the saint.

Anthony spent the remaining years of his life in Padua, and in 1231, after a brief illness, the holy friar passed to his eternal reward at the age of thirty-six. Pope Gregory IX canonized Anthony within a year of his death. Anthony's preaching reputation increased after his death when his tomb was opened, thirty years later, and his tongue was found incorrupt. The holy Franciscan friar is remembered on the Church's liturgical calendar on June 13 and is often invoked as the patron saint of lost items.

A Spiritual Revolution

Beginning in the thirteenth century, the Church witnessed intense spiritual activity with the rise of mystical movements, new forms of piety and popular devotion, and the mendicant, or begging, friars.[12] The new religious orders of mendicants supported the papacy during the reform movement and in its fight against secular interference. Those drawn to this new way of monastic living, a life that was active in the urban areas of the world and contemplative in community, were motivated by a desire to live the Faith in a radical way. In an age when the Church was wealthy, these new orders embraced holy poverty and became the first groups to exist literally by begging. The new orders initiated a revolution in the clergy.

The two founders of these new radical mendicant religious orders became conscious, through the action of the Holy Spirit, of their mission in the same year. One was given twenty years to launch his work; the other only fifteen. Together, these two men changed the Church and the world.

Francis of Assisi (ca. 1181/2–1226)

Pietro and Pica Bernardone baptized their infant with the name Giovanni, but his father called him Francesco (Francis) due to Pietro's fondness for France, where he traveled frequently for business. Francis lived a carefree life and was something of a "party boy" in adolescence. In his early twenties Francis went to war against neighboring Perugia. Assisi lost the Battle of Collestrada, and Francis was captured. His imprisonment for a year by the Perugians changed Francis's life.

The previously carefree young man with a focus on the world became spiritual and prayerful, with a concern for the poor. He made a pilgrimage to Rome. Later, in 1205, he received a vision in the dilapidated church of San Damiano (St. Peter Damian). Francis witnessed the crucifix in the downtrodden church come alive and say to him, "Francis, go, repair my house, which, as you can see, is falling completely to ruin."[13] At first, Francis took the vision literally and provided resources to rebuild the little church. Later, he came to understand the vision was meant in a wider sense, encompassing the spiritual renewal of the universal Church.

Over the next few years, Francis continued to change his way of life. His concern for spiritual matters greatly angered his father. In 1208, Francis decided to fully embrace "Lady Poverty" by renouncing his wealth in a publicly dramatic fashion: "He stripped off all of his clothes and gave them back to his father. He didn't even keep his undergarments, but stripped himself stark naked before all the bystanders. The bishop, amazed at his boldness and passion, took Francis into his arms and covered him."[14]

His way of life and emphasis on personal sanctification attracted others, and eventually Francis decided to seek approval for the group from the pope. According to tradition, Pope Innocent III granted Francis and his group the ability to preach after having a dream: in the pontiff's dream, he watched in horror as his cathedral, the Lateran basilica, swayed on the point of collapse—but was saved when a little man placed his shoulder to the church to stop its destruction. When Francis appeared before the pope, Innocent recognized Francis as the man from his dream.

The holy man from Assisi was ordained a deacon and wrote the first Rule for his little group. Francis wanted his followers to engage in three works: preaching, begging, and service to the poor. The Franciscans preached in the vernacular and carried the Gospel to the people with the simple theme of imitating the life of Christ. The group preached only with permission from local bishops and focused on Christian joy, embracing poverty, and concern for one's neighbor, especially the poor, and always with "total fidelity to orthodox doctrine."[15]

Francis expected his followers to radically embrace poverty, writing in the Rule, "I expressly forbid any brother to accept money in any way whatsoever, whether in person or through a third party."[16] Francis extolled poverty not for its own sake but because total detachment from material things helped the Christian on the path of salvation by imitating Christ. The embrace of radical poverty is difficult, and Francis told those who were too ashamed to beg "that whenever . . . they asked a person for alms, they were actually performing an act of charity, because that person now had an opportunity to do a good work."[17]

Besides the three works of preaching, begging, and serving the poor, Francis desired to evangelize the world through missionary efforts. He had a special desire to bring the Gospel to Muslims. He set out to reach the Middle East in 1212, but his ship ran afoul of the weather and he was forced to turn back. A year later he decided to travel to Morocco for the same purpose, but while traveling in Spain, the holy man became ill and had to cancel his trip. Eventually, in 1219, Francis and several companions arrived at the crusader camp in Damietta, Egypt, where he preached the Gospel to the sultan al-Kamil (see this chapter's You Be the Judge feature).

Franciscans were missionaries not only in non-Christian lands but also in other parts of Christendom. In 1219, one group of sixty friars led by John of Parma traveled to German territory. The men did not know the language but soon discovered the word *ja* and the reaction it brought from the natives when they used it to answer questions. However, the word brought a different reaction when asked if they were heretics. When they answered *ja*, they were arrested and thrown into prison![18]

After his failed evangelization mission during the Fifth Crusade, Francis traveled to the Holy Land. His experience on the crusade and in the Latin East prompted the friar in 1221 to incorporate a chapter on relations with Islam in his revised Rule for the order. The chapter emphasized the importance of evangelizing Muslims by an authentic Christian witness, proclamation of the Word of God, and martyrdom.

Closer to home, Francis devised an ingenious way to evangelize and catechize Christians during Advent in preparation for the celebration of the Nativity of the Lord. At a church in the town of Greccio in 1223 (central Italy, about sixty miles north of Rome), the little holy man created the first crèche: "I wish to do something that will recall to memory the little Child who was born in Bethlehem and set before our bodily eyes in some way the inconveniences of his infant needs."[19]

A year after creating the crèche at Greccio, Francis received a vision and a special gift from the Lord:

> In this vision he saw a man in the form of a seraph, or angel with six wings, standing over him with hands outstretched and feet together fixed on a cross. Marks of nails began to appear on his hands and feet, just as he had seen a minute before on the crucified man standing over him. His right side, also, looked like it had been pierced with a spear, and was covered with a scar, and was bleeding so much that his tunic and clothing were covered.[20]

The wounds of Christ, known as the stigmata, affected Francis for the remaining two years of his life. His stigmata are among the most well-known cases of the phenomenon in Church history but were not the first. In the eleventh century, St. Peter Damian recorded the story of a holy man prone to extreme penances, who received the unique gift of suffering with the wounds of the Lord.

Physically beaten from a life of penances, travels, and stress, *il poverello*, the little poor man of Assisi, reached the end of his earthly life in 1226 at the age of forty-six. His holiness and reputation were so well known and admired that Pope Gregory IX canonized him only two years after his death. Holiness attracts, and Francis's order had grown quickly, reaching five thousand members in 1220. By the end of the thirteenth century, there were twenty-five thousand Franciscans in 1,100 houses throughout Christendom.[21]

Dominic of Castile (1170–1221)

The other important religious founder of the thirteenth century, Dominic, was born into a saintly Castilian family. Pope Leo XII (r. 1823–1829) beatified his mother, Joanna of Aza, in 1828, and his brother, Manes, received the same recognition by Pope Gregory XVI (r. 1831–1846). Dominic spent his early life in schools and universities, a time that served him well in his future endeavors. During his time at the University of Palencia, the pious student sold all his theology books to benefit the poor, saying, "Would you have me study off these dead skins, when men are dying of hunger?"[22]

The student became a priest and continued to perform pious actions such as refusing to sleep in a bed and walking barefoot. Concerned about the plight of fellow Christians held captive by Muslims, Dominic twice attempted to sell himself into slavery to free them. His piety and intellectual skills came to the attention of Bishop Diego of Osma, who made the young man his assistant.

In 1203, Alfonso IX, king of Castile, sent Bishop Diego and his assistant on a mission to a foreign nobleman to secure marriage for his son, Prince Ferdinand. The pair traveled through southern France and encountered the Albigensian heresy sweeping through the region. The nobleman agreed to allow his daughter to marry the Castilian prince, so the bishop, his assistant, and the young lady began the journey to Castile. Sadly, the young woman died on the trip.

Free from their royal mission, Bishop Diego and Dominic traveled to Rome and met Pope Innocent III, who sent them to southern France to combat the Albigensian heresy. Dominic recognized that the heresy spread because the local Catholic clergy were, at best, not given the educational skills needed to successfully debate the educated heretics and, at worst, completely ignorant of the Faith. Dominic also saw firsthand the negative effects of a clergy that did not live the virtues, especially chastity. Dominic was very active in France during most of the Albigensian Crusade. He befriended Simon de Montfort, the leader of the crusade, until his death in 1218, and prayed before the victory of Catholic forces at the Battle of Muret in September 1213.

It was during his time in Languedoc that Dominic became aware of his special calling and the needs of the Church. In the year 1215, Dominic founded the Order of Preachers, a mendicant group of clergy dedicated to preaching, combatting heresy, education, and imitating Christ in poverty. Dominic wanted his brothers to fight the "peril of complacency, of intellectual routine, of ignorance which opens the door to doctrinal error."[23] Pope Honorius III approved the new order in 1216 and gave the friars a universal preaching mission. Dominic was appointed Master of the Sacred Palace (the pope's theologian) the following year and spent the remainder of his life dedicated to the order, especially founding houses of study for his friars at the universities of Europe. The order spread rapidly as its reputation for holiness and intellectual pursuits increased throughout Christendom; by the early fourteenth century, there were twelve thousand members, including two popes (Bl. Innocent V and Bl. Benedict XI).[24] The saintly preacher died in Bologna in 1221. Gregory IX canonized him in 1234.

With the foundation of their new religious orders, Francis and Dominic changed the Church and the world in the thirteenth century. Their revolution in the spiritual life stressed holy poverty in imitation of Christ. Forgoing the cares of the world by complete abandonment to divine providence, the friars of Francis and Dominic were able to focus solely on their charisms of preaching, service to the poor, and combatting heresy.

YOU BE THE JUDGE:

Was St. Francis a radical lover of animals and flowers?

There are many stories and legends surrounding St. Francis's love for God's creation. There is the episode at Gubbio where he instructed the people to feed hungry "brother Wolf," who was eating their flock, rather than be angry with him. There are tales of Francis preaching to attentive birds. Francis's love for created beings was rooted in a deep love of Christ and recognition of the presence of God in the world, which is reflected in the famous prayer/poem he wrote in 1225, *The Canticle of the Sun*.

Some in the modern age have exaggerated Francis's love for nature and all God's creatures and have co-opted him for their own agendas. Although Francis was concerned about animals and flowers, he was more concerned with the task of evangelization, especially of the Muslim world. The holy man attempted several journeys to Islamic territory to preach the Gospel until his successful effort during the Fifth Crusade in Egypt.

Francis and his twelve companions arrived at the crusader camp outside Damietta in late summer 1219. Francis discussed his desire to convert sultan al-Kamil with the crusade leader, Cardinal Pelagius, but the cleric urged him to abandon such plans. Despite the protestations of the cardinal, Francis and the friar Illuminato "set out towards the enemy lines, singing. . . . To comfort his less reassured companion, Francis showed him two ewes peacefully grazing in this perilous spot. 'Courage, Brother!' he cried joyously. 'Put your trust in Him who sends us forth like sheep in the midst of wolves'" (Omar Englebert, *St. Francis of Assisi*, 236, quoted in Carroll, *Glory of Christendom*, 197). When Francis and his fellow friar reached the Muslim lines, they were taken into custody, beaten, and chained. Brought before al-Kamil, Francis preached the Gospel for several days to the sultan, who listened attentively. Despite Francis's preaching and heroic journey, al-Kamil did not convert, but when sending Francis back to the crusader lines, he asked the saint to "remember me in your prayers, and may God, by your intercession, reveal to me which belief is more pleasing to Him" (Englebert, *St. Francis of Assisi*, 236–40, quoted in Carroll, *Glory of Christendom*, 197).

Francis's deep love of Christ and his concern for the salvation of all souls led him to focus the efforts of his order on preaching the Gospel. Although he loved all of God's creatures and his creation, these were never ends in themselves. For Francis, creation was a reflection of God's presence in the world and worthy of respect, but not at the expense of his true mission of evangelization.

Chapter 8

Medieval Inquisitors and Scholars

C hristendom saw in heresy the specter of its own destruction; for to embrace heresy is to mutilate the figure of Christ, to parody the Church's teaching, to misunderstand the authority of God present in His Church, to inflict a mortal wound upon society, and to imperil the whole Christian world.

—Henri Daniel-Rops[1]

Church history is rife with the emergence and reemergence of various heretical beliefs, and the Middle Ages was not immune from this pattern. In the early eleventh century, a heresy appeared in southern France. The heresy was reminiscent of Gnosticism during the early Church's history. Gnostics believed that material and spiritual things were in a state of constant war and that material things were bad and the creation of an evil god, whereas spiritual things were good and created by a benevolent god. St. Irenaeus of Lyons (140–202) combatted the falsehoods of the Gnostics, as did St. Augustine (354–430) later in the fourth century when the heresy morphed into Manicheanism.

The Church initially dealt with the resurgence of these heretical teachings in southern France through local councils at Toulouse (1119) and Tours (1163), where condemnations were issued. Despite the censures, however, the heresy spread rapidly, especially in the region of Albi, from which the heresy took its name: Albigensianism. It was also known as Catharism (from the Greek *katharos*, meaning "clean or pure") because the heretics taught they held to the "pure" teaching of Jesus, uncorrupted by the Church. The Church carried on a patient campaign against the heresy for sixty years before it became apparent that more extreme measures were necessary.

Southern France in the Thirteenth Century

Languedoc, the region in southern France, was unique in the medieval period. The area was not royal territory, and the French king had extremely limited power over it. The people of Languedoc spoke a different language than the northern French; the dialect was closer to Castilian in neighboring Spain. The region was also more urbanized than northern France, and its towns were run by councils of citizens that were more powerful than the secular nobility. The Church in the region suffered from corrupt, worldly, ignorant, illiterate, and unchaste clerics who were inadequate to stop the spread of the heresy that inflamed the land. The bishops were guilty of simony and absenteeism. Pope Innocent III described the region's bishops in a biting rebuke of their behavior:

> [The bishops were] blind men, dumb dogs who can no longer bark . . . men who will do anything for money. All of them, from the greatest to the least are zealous in avarice, lovers of gifts, seekers of rewards. Through such men the name of the Lord is blasphemed. . . . They say the good is bad and the bad is good; they turn light into darkness and darkness into light, sweet to bitter and bitter to sweet. They do not fear God nor respect man. . . . They give church offices to illiterate boys whose behavior is often scandalous.[2]

With such bad examples from the Catholic clergy, it's not surprising that a heretical movement with leaders who actually practiced what they preached spread rapidly in the region. Another contributing factor to the widespread acceptance of the heresy was the general indifference to the threat of heresy in Languedoc, as contrasted with the rest of Christendom. In southern France, heretics and Catholics lived peacefully together, and the clergy numbered heretics among their family members and friends.

Embracing heresy resulted in no serious social or political ramifications in the region, unlike other areas of Christian Europe.

The Medieval View of Heresy

The people of Christendom in the Middle Ages did not view different religious ideas as matters of opinion. Instead, they demanded the eradication of heresy since it posed an active threat to the souls of the faithful and to the peace and security of society. In addition, heresy often produced violence, which led secular rulers to punish it with stiff penalties (death), since they were charged with maintaining peace and security in society. As a result, secular rulers usually dealt swiftly with any false teachings in their territories. In contrast, the Church focused on eternal punishment and a desire for the conversion and repentance of heretics for the sake of their salvation and expected secular authorities to combat heresy in order to prevent people from placing their souls in jeopardy.

Up Close and Personal:
BERNARD GUI (1261–1331)

The Frenchman Bernard Guidonis (usually shortened to Gui) was a brilliant theologian, historian, bishop, and inquisitor. Bernard entered the Order of Preachers and spent fifteen years as a teacher. He became a lecturer in theology at the Dominican convent in Albi, the main battleground between the Church and a pernicious heresy.

Appointed inquisitor, Bernard spent the next several decades prosecuting heretics, including Albigensians, Waldensians, the False Apostles, and the Fraticelli. His experiences led him to write a manual for inquisitors known as the *Practica*. In his work, Bernard stressed that the inquisitor should be in control of his emotions, resolute, free from malice and anger, wary of laziness and gullibility, imbued with a spirit of compassion, and not motivated by cruelty. Bernard embodied these attributes and was known as just and merciful.

In his book *The Waldensian Heretics*, Bernard provided keen insight, derived from personal experience, into dealing with these heretics. The group was named for Peter Waldo of Lyons, a successful merchant who, in 1170, decided to sell his goods, give to the poor, and abandon his family. His message attracted followers, and those who joined him began calling themselves the Humiliati, or the Poor Men of Lyons. The group taught contempt for Church authority, denied the Real Presence of Christ in the Eucharist, forbade the taking of oaths, and argued against the death penalty as criminal punishment. Bernard gave a written example of an interrogation with these wily heretics:

> Asked about the faith which he holds and believes, he answers, "I believe everything that a good Christian ought to believe." Questioned as to whom he considers a good Christian, he replies, "He who believes as Holy Church teaches him to believe." When he is asked what he means by "Holy Church," he answers, "My lord, that which you say and believe is the Holy Church." If you say to him, "I believe that the Holy Church is the Roman Church, over which the lord pope rules; and under him, the prelates," he replies, "I believe it." Meaning that he believes that you believe it. (Bernard Gui, *The Waldensian Heretics*, quoted in Ross and McLaughlin, *Portable Medieval Reader*, 202–16)

During his long tenure as an inquisitor, Bernard issued 930 judgments in heresy cases and only remanded forty-two obstinate heretics to the state for punishment. (See Dawson, *Formation of Christendom*, 234; and Walsh, *Characters of the Inquisition*, 55.) Bernard illustrated the main focus of the medieval inquisitors was the salvation of the soul of those who

embraced false teachings through a patient and charitable investigation. As a reward for his service to the Church, Pope John
XXII (r. 1316–1334) made Bernard a bishop. The celebrated Bernard Gui died at the age of seventy in 1331.

Albigensianism (Catharism)

The Cathari believed in a dualistic system of goodness and evil predi-
cated upon spirit and matter as opposing principles. They saw the world
as the stage of conflict between the god of light and spiritual things and
the god of darkness and material things. The Cathari taught that Satan
created the first man and woman from material elements alone and did
not infuse their material body with souls. The god of light took pity upon
Adam and Eve and gave them souls, but they rebelled by engaging in the
sexual act, which imprisoned a good spiritual soul in the bad material
body of a baby. Heterosexual intercourse was viewed as the greatest sin
in Cathari morality, and strict believers were obliged to forgo marriage.
If tempted sexually, allowance was made for homosexuality and bestiality
in order that procreation would not result.[3] In Cathari theology, God sent
Jesus to humanity to illustrate how to escape the power of Satan. Jesus was
neither God nor man but rather a phantom that appeared on the earth.
He preached spiritual release so that the soul could be freed from the
confines of the evil prison of the body. The Catholic Church, which was
the creation of Satan, had distorted Jesus' original message. The Cathari
believed they possessed the secret original knowledge of Jesus that could
be learned only through membership in the Cathar "church."

The leaders of this movement were known as the Perfect, who had
renounced the world in a solemn public ceremony known as the *consolamentum*, which was akin to baptism and ordination. The Perfect were
required to abstain from eating meat, eggs, and any food derived from
animal sexual intercourse (except fish), and they practiced extreme fasting.

A majority of the Perfect were women, and nearly a third were members of the nobility.[4] Cathari regarded the highest form of worship to be suicide as a result of the *endura* or death by starvation. Sometimes, however, suicide was accomplished through the use of poison, voluntarily contracting pneumonia, or exposure.[5] They believed that suicide freed the good spiritual soul from the confines of the evil material body.

Most adherents of the heresy were known as "believers" who, unlike the Perfect, could eat meat, marry, and engage in sexual activity. In order to hide their heretical behavior, believers were allowed to continue to receive Catholic sacraments, but they could not take oaths or perform military service. Many believers waited until near death to take the *consolamentum* and become Perfect.

The appearance of holiness in the Perfect helped spread the dangerous heresy in Languedoc. Their austere life contrasted sharply with the greed, corruption, and lack of virtue displayed by the Catholic clergy in the area. Priests were ignorant of the Faith and could not successfully defend the Church from the criticism of the Cathari, even if they wanted to do so. Pope Innocent III began a process of needed reform in the region by removing incompetent and immoral bishops and sent Pierre de Castlenau, a Cistercian monk with a reputation of holiness, on a mission to the area to convert the heretics and motivate the nobility to combat heresy.

Count Raymond VI of Toulouse (1156–1222) was the most important secular ruler in Languedoc. Unfortunately, Raymond VI was nothing like his great-grandfather, the famous Raymond IV of the First Crusade. He was skeptical, conniving, carnal, impetuous, and not concerned about the dangerous heresy sweeping his territory. In his capacity as papal legate, Pierre de Castlenau excommunicated Raymond in 1207 and placed his lands under interdict for his failures to stem the Albigensian heresy.

The following year the two men met in an attempt to restore communion, but the meeting was not cordial. Raymond threatened the pope's representative, saying, "Wherever you go, whether by land or by water, take care: I shall be watching you!"[6] The next morning in very mysterious circumstances, Pierre de Castlenau was murdered. News of his legate's death infuriated Pope Innocent III, who absolved all subjects from their oaths of fealty to Raymond and urged them to "proceed against his person, and even to occupy and hold his land."[7] A few months later, the pope declared Raymond a murderer and a heretic and called a crusade to eradicate the pernicious heresy from southern France.

The Albigensian Crusade

The Albigensian Crusade occurred only after the Church had carried on a patient, nonviolent campaign to preserve the unity of the faith in Languedoc and protect the eternal souls of its inhabitants. Sadly, violent means were seen as the only remaining option. Even more unfortunate was the bitter nature of the conflict. The crusade was, in reality, a nasty twenty-year civil war that ultimately destroyed the independence of the region and increased royal control.

Innocent recognized that crusading in southern France was quite different from a campaign to the Holy Land, so he introduced several innovations to the crusading movement. Warriors pledged forty days of service to the crusade, which was the same number of days of annual military service they owed to their lords. This innovation produced the positive effect of generating sufficient manpower, but the constant departure and arrival of troops also brought forth the unintended consequence of stalling the crusade.

Simon de Montfort (d. 1218), an accomplished warrior who had left the Fourth Crusade before the capture of Zara, led the army. The campaign against the heretics achieved results in its first year (1209) through a series of sieges and the capture of strategic towns. Simon's army won a significant victory at the Battle of Muret on September 12, 1213, despite being severely outnumbered by the forces of King Peter II of Aragon (r. 1196–1213), who had come to the aid of his brother-in-law Raymond VI. Simon's troops, with prayers from St. Dominic, succeeded in defeating the foreign army and Peter II was killed.

Simon's victory established his reign as count of Toulouse, but within a few years a rebellion was led by the son of Raymond VI. The rebellion succeeded in recapturing territory and was bolstered when Simon de Montfort was killed at the siege of Toulouse in the summer of 1218. A stone from a mangonel, a siege engine that flung projectiles from a sling, reportedly struck him on the head. The crusade ended with the involvement of King Louis VIII and the French royal army. A few years later, Raymond VII (r. 1222–1249) made a public act of penance and was absolved, reconciled to the Church, and subsequently recognized as the legitimate count of Toulouse.

Although the crusade was over, the heresy lingered. The brutal fighting of the civil war masquerading as the Albigensian Crusade strengthened the rule of the king in southern France. While it dealt a significant blow to the Cathari movement, the false teaching persisted. This is what led to the rise of the medieval inquisitors.

A Legal Revolution

Twelfth-century Christendom witnessed the rediscovery and revival of imperial Roman law, which produced a revolution in legal process and application. This revival was one of the most significant events in the intellectual and institutional development of medieval Europe.[8] The first universal collection of Church (canon) law was Gratian's *Decretum*, compiled in the 1140s at Bologna. The next century saw the work of the Dominican canonist St. Raymond of Peñafort (ca. 1175–1275), who added to the *Decretum* in his work *Liber Extra*.[9]

Besides the formation of a universal canon law, the most significant change in legal process involved replacing the *accusatorial* procedure with the *inquisitorial* procedure. Before the twelfth century, the prosecution of criminal actions was a private matter. Secular authorities did not investigate and prosecute criminal actions. Instead, a victim or their family approached the secular lord and demanded action by accusing the alleged perpetrator and swearing an oath. The accused was brought before the lord and took an oath proclaiming their innocence.[10] The lord passed judgment on who was telling the truth. Sometimes, the accused underwent ordeals, such as thrusting one's hand into boiling water or picking up a hot iron, or judicial combat.[11] Because medieval people believed firmly in the judgment of God, if an accused party died as a result of a judicial combat, that was seen as proof of his guilt. Inquisitorial procedure involved the direct action of competent authority who initiated criminal investigations comprising the collection of evidence and witness testimony, which required two eye-witnesses, or the confession of the accused.[12] The end result of the inquisitorial process was an official judgment and punishment.

Medieval Inquisitors

The development of what many people know as "the Inquisition" occurred over the course of several papacies and stretched beyond the medieval period. In 1184, Pope Lucius III (r. 1181–1185), in *Ad abolendam*, sent a list of heresies to the bishops of the Church and ordered them to take an active role in determining the guilt of accused heretics. Now trained theologians using the inquisitorial process were required to examine the accused. Secular lords had previously borne the responsibility of prosecuting heresy in their territories, but the Church became concerned about the violence with which secular rulers, using theologically untrained individuals, engaged in that activity. Fifteen years later, Pope Innocent III issued *Vergentis in senium*, which defined heretics as traitors to God. This allowed secular authorities to punish convicted heretics. Treason in secular courts was punished by confiscation of property and death. That motivated Pope Gregory IX in 1231 to formally institute the procedures for medieval inquisitors to prosecute heresy. His establishment of the medieval inquisitors in *Ille humani generis* was a matter of charity designed to save the soul of the heretic and a measure of protection for the unity of the Church and society. Heresy, after all, disrupted the unified fabric of Christendom.

Secular authorities, however, were not trained to adequately assess heresy. As a result, the Church turned to medieval inquisitors, many of whom were Dominicans trained in theology, canon law, and philosophy, to protect the Church and society from the evil of heresy. Inquisitors desired the conversion and repentance of accused heretics for the sake of their salvation and took pains to provide multiple opportunities for confession and reconciliation.

Obstinate heretics were remanded to the state for the secular punishment of heresy, which was death. Inquisitors could investigate and prosecute only baptized Christians as heresy was a postbaptismal denial of a doctrine of the Church. The inquisitors had no jurisdiction over Jews or Muslims.

Inquisitorial Procedure

Medieval inquisitors, and even the later institutional tribunals known as Inquisitions, followed established procedures in the investigation of heresy. In the medieval period, inquisitors were itinerant, traveling to areas where heresy was reported. They gathered the clergy and people and preached a sermon on the importance of salvation, truth, and the doctrines of the Church. An "edict of grace" was granted for a period of fifteen to forty days, which allowed voluntary confession of heresy, reconciliation, and a suitable penance.

After the period of grace was over, accusations from others were allowed and the inquisitors began the trial process. The accused came before the inquisitors and were asked questions about their beliefs. A written record was kept of the deliberations, and witnesses were called to give testimony about the accused and their heretical beliefs and practices. The accused was afforded the opportunity to call favorable witnesses and cross-examine hostile ones as well as provide a list of enemies, whose testimony was discounted. The trial consisted mostly of questions and answers of the accused and witnesses with the inquisitors endeavoring to illustrate to the accused the error of their belief with an emphasis on catechesis and an explanation of Catholic doctrine.

After 1252, recourse to torture was authorized as a means to elicit a confession from the accused. Although torture was routine in secular courts, its use by medieval inquisitors was rare, as most (rightly) believed it ineffective. Torture was allowed only when the inquisitor believed the accused was hiding the truth and when all other means of eliciting a confession had failed. Its use was governed by a series of strict procedures (see You Be the Judge feature in this chapter). At the end of the trial phase, the inquisitors passed sentence on the accused after presenting evidence to a

large jury. The jury was comprised of usually no fewer than twenty prominent men from the community, who reviewed the case and recommended
a sentence, which the inquisitor was under no obligation to accept.[13]

Heretics who confessed and sought reconciliation were given penances
such as fasting, prayers, and sometimes the wearing of yellow crosses on
their garments for a time, and wealthy heretics were told to provide money
for the building of churches or giving alms. Some repentant heretics were
given the penance of pilgrimage to a particular shrine or even taking the
cross to go on crusade. Although the sentences may seem harsh to people
in today's world, ecclesiastical courts were known as fair and just bodies
as compared to secular courts.

When it came to Catharism, the medieval inquisitors succeeded where
the bloody civil war of the Albigensian Crusade failed. By the middle of
the fourteenth century, Catharism had ceased to exist. Heresy threatened the fabric of medieval society and jeopardized the eternal salvation
of the heretic and those who embraced his false teachings. The medieval
inquisitors sought the reconciliation of heretics, not their torture or death,
and the protection of the Church and the people at a time when the Faith
occupied a preeminent place in society.

Medieval Scholars

The medieval inquisitors would not have existed without the creation
of the unique institution of the university. Prior to the eleventh century,
formal education occurred mostly in monasteries and their associated
schools with a focused curriculum on biblical theology and sacred scripture. In the Carolingian empire of the eighth and ninth centuries, palace schools were created and foreign scholars were recruited to teach the
standardized curriculum, encompassing the *trivium* (grammar, logic,
and rhetoric) and the *quadrivium* (arithmetic, geometry, astronomy, and
music) of Alcuin of York (ca. 732–804).

In the eleventh century, schools attached to cathedrals became the
center of formal education. These schools were open to boys and girls,

and instruction in the *trivium* and *quadrivium* was given with no tuition, although wealthy families were expected to pay something. In the early twelfth century, France counted fifty cathedral schools.[14]

In the mid-twelfth century, universities were established at Paris and Bologna, and soon this "community of teachers and scholars" (*universitas magistrorum et scholarium*, from which the name "university" is derived) spread throughout Christendom.[15] Pope Gregory IX issued *Parens Scientiarum* in 1231, making the University of Paris, with an enrollment of more than a thousand students from across Christendom, an international association responsible to the pope.[16] Pope Innocent IV (r. 1243–1254) described the universities as "rivers of science, which water and make fertile the soil of the universal Church."[17] The community of teachers and scholars was organized into the four faculties of theology, law, medicine, and the arts, and teaching was conducted in the three stages of *lectio* (reading a text), *quaestio* (commentary on the text), and *disputatio* (critical analysis of the text's thesis).[18]

One thinker who had a profound impact on universities, although he never taught in one, was St. Anselm of Canterbury (1033–1109). In his late twenties, Anselm entered the Benedictine order and was ordained a priest. Later, he was appointed prior of the monastery of Bec in Normandy, became abbot, and in 1094 was made archbishop of Canterbury in England. Anselm had a brilliant intellect and recognized the harmonious relationship between faith and reason, as expressed in his famous dictum *fides quaerens intellectum* (faith seeking understanding). Anselm believed the investigation of knowledge must begin with faith, from which understanding of the world was derived and not vice versa. He wrote several famous treatises including *Cur Deus Homo* (Why God Became Man), and the *Proslogion*, a work proving the existence of God ("God is that than which nothing greater can be thought"). His incorporation of Aristotelian philosophy with sacred theology has earned him the appellation "Father of Scholasticism." It was Anselm who laid the foundation for the medieval scholastics and their method of learning.

Peter Abelard (1079–1142) was perhaps the first celebrity professor. A man with a penetrating, intense, speculative, and radical mind, Abelard taught thousands of students at the cathedral school in Paris, including future bishops, cardinals, and a pope.[19] Abelard's teaching departed from Anselm's dictum by stressing understanding (and not faith) as the foundation of knowledge. He was known for pushing the established boundaries of both theology and philosophy. Abelard's private life was as calamitous as his teaching. Abelard fell in love with Heloise, a young woman he tutored, fathered a child with her, and then secretly married. Their love letters are some of the most exquisite writings of the medieval period. Eventually, the scandal forced the pair into monastic life with Abelard at the Abbey of St. Denis near Paris and Heloise at a convent in nearby Argenteuil.

Abelard's speculative teaching placed him in danger of heresy and drew the criticism of St. Bernard of Clairvaux in his work *Tract on the Errors of Abelard*, in which the holy Cistercian wrote, "He [Abelard] defines faith as opinion; as if, indeed, a man were at liberty to think and talk about it as he liked! As if the sacred things of our faith depended on vague surmise and were not founded on the solid basis of truth."[20] Pope Innocent II (r. 1130–1143) convicted Abelard of heresy, excommunicated and silenced him, and ordered his objectionable works burned.

Abelard sought refuge at the monastery of Cluny. Peter the Venerable, Cluny's abbot, convinced the pope to withdraw the excommunication. Abelard made peace with Bernard and wrote a recantation and profession of faith: "I renounce the title of philosopher. . . . I do not wish to be an Aristotle if that means being separated from Christ."[21] He lived his remaining brief time as a humble monk and died in 1142.

Peter Lombard (d. 1160) was another scholar who taught at the cathedral school in Paris and achieved universal recognition for his work *Book on Sentences*, which was a collection of the teachings of theologians and Church Fathers. The work was organized into four books covering the topics of the Trinity, creation, sin and grace, the Incarnation and redemption of man, the sacraments, and last things. Peter's *Sentences* became the standard university theological textbook for centuries.

Building on the work of St. Anselm, Peter Abelard, and Peter Lombard, a fresh crop of scholars in the thirteenth century developed a new method of teaching and investigation of knowledge. Known as scholasticism, this pedagogy focused on developing precise definitions and reasoning through questions. The scholastics synthesized theology, scripture, and Aristotelian philosophy. St. Bonaventure (1221–1274) and St. Thomas Aquinas (1225–1274) were two of the most influential scholastics and as contemporaries provided the Church with a powerful witness of faithful theologians.

Giovanni di Fidanza joined the Franciscans at the age of seventeen and was known as Bonaventure. He studied at the University of Paris, along with the Dominican Thomas Aquinas, and received his doctorate in theology (on the same day as Aquinas). Bonaventure's scholarly interests were centered on mysticism and the soul's ascent to God. He left the academic world to become the seventh minister general of the Friars Minor at a time when the order was engaged in internal conflict on how to live the Rule of St. Francis. Pope Bl. Gregory X (r. 1271–1276) created Bonaventure a cardinal and requested his assistance at the Second Ecumenical Council of Lyons. Shortly after the completion of the council, Bonaventure died. The holy Franciscan scholar was canonized in 1482 and declared a Doctor of the Church in 1588.

The great Dominican theologian Thomas Aquinas came from a noble family, with relatives occupying positions in the Church and military. His family chose a career in the Church for young Thomas, whose intellect shone forth at an early age. Sent to university in Naples, Thomas was a brilliant student and quickly surpassed the knowledge of his teachers. Sometime in the 1240s, Thomas entered the Order of Preachers, much to the chagrin of his family, who actually kidnapped the young man and held him in captivity for two years in an attempt to convince him to leave the order.

The Dominicans sent Thomas to Paris and Cologne to study under the master scholar St. Albert the Great (ca. 1206–1280). Thomas earned his doctorate in theology and began teaching and writing. His famous work, the *Summa Theologiae*, was written as a guide for students beginning advance work in theology. It comprised three parts on God, the rational creature's advance toward God, and Christ, who is the way to God.

Although Thomas was known for his great intellect and writings, he was a humble and pious friar with a great devotion to the Real Presence of Jesus in the Eucharist. His devotion to the Blessed Sacrament moved him to write the beautiful eucharistic hymns of Benediction, *"Pange Lingua"* (*"Tantum Ergo"*) and *"O, Salutaris Hostia,"* which we still sing today. A year before his death, Thomas told his secretary, Reginald, that during the celebration of Mass, he experienced a supernatural revelation of heaven in which he came to understand that everything he had written was "worthless."[22] Summoned to attend the Second Ecumenical Council of Lyons in 1274, Thomas died on the journey at the age of forty-nine. The Church had not witnessed a great mind such as Thomas Aquinas since St. Augustine, and his writings profoundly influenced theology and Christian philosophy to the present day. Thomas was canonized in 1323 and declared a Doctor of the Church in 1567.

YOU BE THE JUDGE:

Were millions of people tortured and killed by the Inquisition?

(Note: This section is adapted from my book The Real Story of Catholic History, 117–22.)

The Church prohibited the use of torture in ecclesial courts for centuries, but the legal revolution of the twelfth century, with its focus on confession, brought its limited use into investigations of heresy. Although torture was part of the ordinary criminal justice process in the secular world, Pope Innocent IV did not approve its use in ecclesial courts investigating heresy until 1252, twenty years after the establishment of the medieval inquisitors.

Although torture was authorized, its use was governed by a series of strict protocols and protections for the accused and was a measure of last resort. Torture was allowed as a means to elicit confession and could be applied only once and for no more than a half hour (Walsh, *Characters of the Inquisition*, 85). Torture was never applied by clerics, but was used by the secular authorities. The accused could appeal the judicial order to use torture, and several groups of people were automatically exempted including children, the elderly, pregnant women, knights, members of the nobility, and in some cases the clergy (Peters, *Torture*, 57). In the hopes of achieving a quick confession without recourse to torture, its instruments were shown to the accused. Pope Clement V modified the rules governing recourse to torture in 1311 by requiring inquisitors who wanted to use torture to receive permission from the local bishop beforehand.

The purpose of the medieval inquisitors was to investigate heresy and, where found, to encourage voluntary confession, repentance, and reconciliation to the Church. Inquisitors failed if the accused persisted in heresy and refused to recant. Obstinate heretics, after repeated opportunities to confess, were remanded to the state for punishment. Heresy was both an ecclesial and secular crime in the medieval world, and the secular punishment for heresy was death. The death sentence was handed down and carried out by the state, not by the Church.

Despite the common perception that millions of people suffered the final torment of burning at the stake, the historical record proves only a small number of people were executed for heresy during the medieval period and even in the later institutional tribunals. For example, of the 44,674 cases brought before the Spanish Inquisition from 1540 to 1700, only 826 obstinate heretics—or 1.8 percent of cases—were remanded to the state for execution (Jaime Contreras and Gustave Henningsen, "Forty-Four Thousand Cases of the Spanish Inquisition (1540–1700): Analysis of a Historical Data Bank," in *The Inquisition in Early Modern Europe: Studies on Sources and Methods*, 100–129).

Chapter 9

Trouble in the Papacy

For ever since Holy Church has aimed more at temporal than at spiritual things, matters have gone from bad to worse.

—*St. Catherine of Siena*[1]

As the thirteenth century closed, a most curious event occurred. The last thirty years of the century witnessed instability in the papacy, with short reigns and long conclaves to choose successors becoming the norm. When Pope Clement IV (r. 1265–1268) died in 1268, the cardinals bickered incessantly and could not decide on a successor. The stalemate lasted more than two years, during which time there was no pope.

When the cardinals gathered once more in 1270, in what many thought the continuation of futility, the people of Viterbo (in central Italy), where the cardinals assembled, took matters into their own hands. The sixteen cardinals were locked in their meeting place and not released in the hope the extreme measure would produce a papal election. However, the obstinate cardinals refused agreement on a candidate, and after waiting a year with no result, the people decided even more extreme measures were in order. The roof to the building was removed when it was raining, so that the cardinals were exposed to the elements. This harsh method finally brought agreement, and three days later Pope Bl. Gregory X (r. 1271–1276) was elected.

Gregory later called the Second Council of Lyons, which mandated the cardinals assemble in *conclave* (literally, "with a key," meaning a place securely closed). The conclave would occur within ten days of the pope's death, accompanied by only one servant to begin the process of electing a successor. If there was no election after three days, the cardinals were restricted to one meal a day for five days, and then only bread and water until a new pope was selected.[2] Interestingly, four of the sixteen cardinals at the conclave in Viterbo were later elected pope (Hadrian V [r. 1276], Nicholas III [r. 1277–1280], Martin IV [r. 1281–1285], and Honorius IV [r. 1285–1287]).[3] Christ established the papacy as a source of unity and stability for the Church, but when disunity and instability reigned in the Petrine office, calamitous events resulted.

The Saintly Pope Who Quit

Eight years before the end of the thirteenth century, Pope Nicholas IV (r. 1288–1292), the first Franciscan pope, died. The short-reigning Hadrian IV had abrogated the stipulations of the Second Council of Lyons concerning papal elections, so the Church once again witnessed a long interregnum because the cardinals failed to agree on a papal candidate. As the interregnum continued into the summer of its second year, an eighty-four-year-old hermit wrote a letter to one of the cardinals. This simple action began one of the most comedic and tragic stories in Church history.

Peter the hermit lived on Mount Morrone in the Apennines of central Italy and was a well-known mystic who attracted a group of hermits to his mountain. In the summer of 1294, deeply disturbed by the lack of a papal election and the detrimental impact the absence of a pope had on the Church, Peter penned a poignant letter to Cardinal Latino Malabranca Orsini. The holy hermit's warning motivated Orsini to read the letter in the conclave and, moved by the Holy Spirit, he proposed Peter Morrone as pope. Perhaps to Orsini's astonishment, the cardinals agreed, and unbeknownst to him, Peter became pope. Of course, Peter's acceptance was necessary, so a motley crew of clerics, soldiers, and others marched to Peter's hermitage to convince the holy man to step into the shoes of the fisherman. Peter initially refused the office, but the group convinced Peter his election was God's will and necessary for the good of the Church. Despite his protestations, Peter acquiesced and was crowned pope in late

August, taking the name Celestine V. Celestine never set foot in Rome, and instead lived at the royal palace of King Charles II (r. 1285–1309) in Naples. Papal absence from Rome was common in the thirteenth century, as several pontiffs lived away from the Eternal City, even for the length of their pontificate.

Although there was much hope placed in the surprise election of the holy hermit, Celestine's pontificate did not produce the desired results. Instead, Celestine and other Church officials quickly recognized that the aged hermit did not have the skills to reign as pope. Peter Morrone lacked the political skill required to be the visible spiritual head of Christendom and a major temporal ruler at the same time. Perhaps Celestine would have been an excellent pope in an age when the successor of St. Peter played primarily a spiritual role in the world, but he did not live in such an age. Rumors circulated that Celestine desired to abdicate and return to his simple life as a hermit, but some questioned if that was even possible. On December 13, 1294, after a nearly five-month pontificate, Celestine V addressed these rumors and questions in a speech to the cardinals:

> I, Celestine V, moved by valid reasons, that is, by humility, by desire for a better life, by a troubled conscience, troubles of body, a lack of knowledge, personal shortcomings, and so that I may then proceed to a life of greater humility, voluntarily and without compunction give up the papacy and renounce its position and dignity, burdens and honors, with full freedom.[4]

After a two-year deadlock, the cardinals, in a moment of inspiration drawn from a compelling letter by a renowned hermit, had elected a pope with great hope. Now, less than half a year later, that pope renounced his office and placed the Church in another precarious position. This time, the cardinals acted swiftly and elected Cardinal Benedict Gaetani, who took the name Boniface VIII (r. 1294–1303), eleven days after Celestine V's shocking abdication. Boniface VIII is remembered as a heroic defender of the Church by some and as a tyrannical cleric by others.

Pope Boniface VIII

The new pope was a lawyer by education and a skilled diplomat by trade, having spent thirty years as a papal legate. He was also the nephew of Pope Alexander IV (r. 1254–1261). Boniface believed it was his solemn duty to protect the Church from secular encroachment and interference, but his dealings with powerful monarchs and nobles lacked charity, which exacerbated situations that could have otherwise been easily diffused.

One humorous anecdote is that Boniface once said he would rather be a dog than a Frenchman, to which his critics argued the statement was heretical since it implied Frenchmen have no souls![5] Boniface's pontificate was not without controversy. Rumors circulated that while cardinal, Boniface had pressured Pope Celestine V to abdicate because he was wary of the hermit-turned-pope's credibility and authority. Soon after his election, Boniface did order Celestine's arrest. The saintly former pope lived nine months in cruel captivity before passing to his eternal reward.

Boniface engaged in a defense of the Church against secular interference of several monarchs, especially from the French king Philip IV, "the Fair" (r. 1285–1314). The grandson of St. Louis IX, Philip imitated his great forebearer in personal faith by attendance at daily Mass and the performance of penances, but his relationship with the Church was more cantankerous. Unlike his saintly grandfather, Philip viewed the monarchy as power, not service, and desired absolute control over France, including the Church. Aiding him in this pursuit was William of Nogaret (1260–1313), a lawyer, royal advisor, and progeny of heretical parents. Nogaret was a consummate sycophant who desired only to increase Philip's power. A contemporary described the minion as "a body without a soul."[6] When conflict arose with the pope, Nogaret was mostly behind the scenes stoking the fire.

The Fourth Lateran Council earlier in the thirteenth century had stipulated that clergy could not pay taxes levied by secular rulers without consulting the pope.[7] But as the century progressed, secular lords—including the kings of England and France—taxed the Church to pay for their wars. In February 1296, Boniface VIII attempted to enforce the decree of the Fourth Lateran Council by issuing the bull *Clericis laicos*. He forbade clerics from paying taxes to secular lords and required papal approval of any tax on the Church levied by a secular ruler. Failure to abide by these stipulations was to result in excommunication, with absolution reserved to the pope.

Boniface failed to distinguish the situation wherein a bishop, holding royal property as a fief, owed taxes legitimately to the king. Receipt of the bull in France was not favorable, and Philip issued his own counter policies. The king forbade the export of money without royal approval, which placed significant Church revenue on hold from transport to Rome, and issued the decree that no foreigners were allowed in France without royal approval, which was an attack on papal legates, who were (mostly) Italian. Philip also arrested a French bishop on charges of blasphemy, heresy, and treason. A secular trial was conducted, and the prelate was convicted and imprisoned. Philip then had the audacity to submit the verdict to Rome for papal approval. Boniface rejected the request and instead demanded the bishop's immediate release.

In order to address the growing hostile situation in France, Boniface ordered all French bishops to attend a council in Rome, but Philip forbade their attendance. In response, Boniface issued the bull *Ausculta fili* (Listen, Son!) in December 1301 rebuking the king—"Let no one persuade you that you have no superior or that you are not subject to the head of the ecclesiastical hierarchy, for he is a fool who thinks so"—and threatened him with excommunication.[8] Philip was incensed and burned the papal document. Royal agents circulated a forged bull in which Boniface was portrayed as trying to control the king.

As the crisis between king and pope continued into the summer of 1302, Boniface threatened radical action: "If the King of France does not behave himself properly, I shall have the unpleasant duty to depose him like a little boy."[9] That same year Boniface issued another bull, *Unam sanctam*, in which he taught there is no salvation outside the Church; the Church has only one visible head, the pope; and temporal authority is exercised in the world by kings but at the will of the priest.[10]

Nogaret recognized that Boniface was a menace to royal desires, so he hatched a plan to seize the pope and force him to abdicate so the king could install a more favorable one. In September 1303, Nogaret assembled a force of 600 cavalry and 1,500 infantry to storm the papal palace in Anagni, Boniface's hometown, where the pope was staying.[11] As the soldiers entered his room, Boniface offered his head in martyrdom but was not killed. Word spread that the pope was held hostage by a rogue force, and two days later, the townspeople of Anagni attacked the palace and freed Boniface. Nogaret fled and escaped to France. Although Nogaret's attack failed in its initial aims, it succeeded ultimately when a month later, suffering the effects of his maltreatment during the brief captivity and the stress of a volatile papacy, Boniface VIII died.

The pontificate of Boniface VIII illustrates that as the fourteenth century dawned, Christendom was in crisis. No longer did kings and lords look to govern the temporal order peacefully with the Church in maintaining a society rooted in Christian virtue. Instead, secular lords separated themselves politically from the pope and reached for a reign of absolute control of their subjects, including the clergy. The Faith and the will of the pope were no longer paramount in the decisions of kings and secular lords.

Up Close and Personal:
ST. BRIDGET OF SWEDEN
(1303–1373)

Bridget was born into a wealthy Scandinavian family and from an early age showed signs of deep piety. She married the nobleman Ulf Gudmarsson in 1316 and ultimately bore him eight children. Their fourth child, Catherine of Sweden (1331–1381), also became a saint.

Nearly twenty-five years into their marriage, Bridget and Ulf made a pilgrimage to Santiago de Compostela. The journey affected them deeply, and they both decided to live in religious community. Ulf entered a monastery but died soon afterward, while Bridget gave her possessions to the poor and lived in a Cistercian monastery but never became a consecrated religious.

Bridget received private revelations and wrote down the conversations she had with Christ, the Blessed Mother, and the saints. From an early age Bridget had a devotion to the Passion of Christ. Later in life, Jesus answered Bridget's long-prayed question concerning the number of times his body was struck during the Passion: 5,480 times. The Lord instructed Bridget to honor these wounds by praying fifteen Our Fathers and Hail Marys along with other prayers every day for a year, which would equate to the wounds (minus the five wounds in his hands, feet, and side, which have a separate devotion).

Bridget founded a religious community in Sweden (known as the Brigittines) but left her native country and settled in Rome. Seeing firsthand the ill effects of the pope's absence during the exile in Avignon, Bridget wrote letters to the popes in Avignon, urging them to return home.

Pope Bl. Urban V (r. 1362–1370) heeded Bridget's urgings to return to Rome in 1367, but his stay was brief. Political instability in Italy and Roman anger at his creation of six new French cardinals prompted his return to Avignon in 1370, where he died three months later. Bridget continued pleading for the popes to return home and only stopped when she passed to her eternal reward in 1373. Pope Boniface IX (r. 1389–1404) canonized Bridget in 1391, and Pope St. John Paul II (1978–2005) named her copatroness of Europe in 1999.

The Pope Moves to France

Boniface's successor, the Dominican Bl. Benedict XI (r. 1303–1304), reigned for less than a year and died the day before he was to excommunicate Nogaret for his role in attacking Boniface VIII. He was the last pope to live in Rome for the next seventy years. The death of Benedict XI brought opportunity to King Philip IV, who earnestly desired a pope amenable to his whims. After a lengthy delay caused in part by disagreement between the French and Italian cardinals, Bertrand de Got, the archbishop of Bordeaux, was elected, taking the name Clement V (r. 1305–1314).

King Philip IV wanted Clement to undertake three actions designed to tighten the king's hold over the papacy. Philip demanded the trial of the dead Boniface VIII, the suppression of the Knights Templar, and the movement of the papal residence to France. Clement agreed to open proceedings against Boniface VIII in 1310, but the pope postponed the proceedings several times and never ruled against Boniface. Clement V opened the ecumenical Council of Vienne in late 1311 to discuss the issue of the Knights Templar.

Several years earlier, Philip illegally arrested the Templars in France and conducted a royal investigation into the order, mostly because he was envious of their material holdings and wealth. Nogaret had developed charges against the famed military religious order, including the crimes of sodomy, blasphemy, and idolatry. Sadly, Clement was powerless to stop the persecution of the knights and allowed their suppression at the Council of Vienne. Although Clement's bull of suppression did not proclaim the guilt or innocence of the Templars, their material wealth was given to the Hospitallers. The Templars throughout Christendom either were imprisoned or joined other orders (although some areas, notably Portugal, refused to obey the bull). Philip had his final revenge on the Templars when he ordered the burning of the order's master, Jacques de Molay, and deputy, Geoffrey de Charnay, in Paris in March 1314. Pope Clement V died a month later, and King Philip followed in November.

Moving to France

A few years after his election, Clement V announced to stunned cardinals that he was transferring the papal residence to Avignon in southern France. The pope arrived at his new residence in March 1309. Although Avignon was papal and not royal territory, the move cast a pall over the papacy.

Popes had chosen not to live in Rome in centuries past. Indeed, popes in the thirteenth century lived in Provence, Viterbo, and Naples. Yet this papal relocation was viewed differently because it was seen as orchestrated and motivated by the dictates of the French king. The popes lived in Avignon for the next seventy years, placing the bishop of Rome outside the Eternal City for 140 years over two centuries. This ecclesiastical abuse known as absenteeism caused significant problems for the Church. Rome had no resident bishop for most of the fourteenth century, which greatly affected the government of the city as basic civic responsibilities were neglected. Although the popes in Avignon were not puppets of the French king, the perception was that they were; this caused a loss of respect for the office. The papacy had been established by Christ to be a source of unity in the Church, but when popes engaged in actions that fueled disunity, evil resulted.

The time in France changed the composition of the papal curia as most officials and cardinals were French. This played a factor in another papal crisis at the end of the century. While living in Avignon, the popes dealt with one of the most significant health crises to afflict Christendom: the great pestilence.

The Black Death

The plague that swept Europe in the fourteenth century changed the history of Christendom and had lasting cultural and religious ramifications.[12] Its devastation on the population, with nearly every country affected, brought thoughts of the end of the world.[13] The death toll was catastrophic: as high as 70 percent in some areas, and an average of 50 percent of Europe's total population.[14] Michele da Piazza, a Franciscan friar in Sicily, described how the plague came to Sicily initially and then spread throughout Europe: "In the month of October in the year of our Lord 1347, around the first of that month, twelve Genoese galleys, fleeing our Lord's wrath, which came down upon them for their misdeeds, put in at a port in the city of Messina. They brought with them a plague."[15]

Plagues had devastated the Western world before, notably the Byzantine Empire in the sixth century, but this new pestilence spread swiftly and killed abundantly. Once infected, an individual experienced an incubation period of two to eight days after which symptoms appeared. Bacteria collected in the lymph nodes (groin, armpits, and neck) and produced painful buboes, or lumps, on the body. High fever, swelling of the lymph nodes, headaches, diarrhea, vomiting, convulsions, dizziness, and delirium could also result. At times, the buboes burst open and released a nasty pus.

Physicians struggled to treat patients infected with the plague, using enemas and bloodletting. Jacme d'Agramont, a Spanish physician and professor at the University of Lerida, wrote the treatise *Regimen of Protection against Epidemics* in April 1348. He recommended the cessation of bathing in order to ward off the plague: "Habitual bathing is also very dangerous, because the bath opens the pores of the body and through these pores corrupt air enters and has a powerful influence upon our body."[16]

Reactions to the plague varied, with some blaming the Jews for the outbreak (see this chapter's You Be the Judge feature). Others fled cities and towns to live in the countryside for the duration of the pestilence. Christendom was affected economically as material shortages occurred due to the disruption of the merchant trade. The loss of population reduced the workforce but had the positive impact of increasing wages and creating a higher standard of living for the remaining workers.[17] The spiritual response to the plague was positive overall as people sought solace through prayer and the sacraments.

The Church was affected significantly since clergy suffered a higher percentage of mortality than the laity as faithful clerics ministered to their flocks in crisis. Nearly 90 percent of urban clergy perished, and 40 percent of all priests in Christendom died.[18] The plague devastated religious orders as well, especially the Franciscans and Dominicans. The plague's impact on the clergy was so severe there was a shortage of priests. This prompted the lowering of the minimum age for ordination, which left the Church with a generation of undereducated and inexperienced clergy.

YOU BE THE JUDGE:

Did the Church blame the Black Death on the Jews?

Sadly, some people, especially in southern France and Spain, did blame the Jewish people for the outbreak of the plague, with tales of well-poisoning and other nefarious plots. The false accusations seemed credible to medieval people living in areas with large Jewish populations and regions with a history of anti-Semitism.

Since Jews appeared not to suffer as high a mortality rate as others, belief that they were responsible for the pestilence was heightened. Of course, the reason Jewish death rates were less than other groups was their segregation in areas away from the high concentration of rodents and their lifestyle choices such as hygiene habits and diet (see Cantor, *In the Wake of the Plague*, 163). Pogroms erupted in the fall of 1348 and quickly spread to nearly a hundred towns and cities, mostly in German areas along the Rhine. Jews were burned, robbed, expelled, and in some cases committed suicide rather than suffer death at the hands of the mob. Konrad of Megenberg reported in his work *Concerning the Mortality in Germany* (ca. 1350), "Sometimes . . . they [Jews] shut themselves up in a house with the doors barred and, after setting the house on fire, they died by their own hands by slitting the throats of their children, along with their own" (quoted in Aberth, *Black Death*, 156).

Although modern critics blame the Church for fostering or even participating in the pogroms, the historical record reflects the opposite reality. Bishops in areas affected tried to protect the Jewish people but were not always successful. Jacob von Königshofen described the abuse inflicted upon the Jewish people on account of the plague but mentions this did not occur "in Avignon, for the pope protected them there" (Jacob von Königshofen, *The Cremation of the Strasbourg Jews*, quoted in Ross and McLaughlin, *Portable Medieval Reader*, 174–75).

Pope Clement VI issued the bull *Sicut Judeis* in July 1348 defending the Jewish people: "We nevertheless are mindful of our duty to shelter the Jews. . . . It has come to our attention by public fame, or rather infamy, that some Christians out of rashness have impiously slain several of the Jews, without respect to age or sex, after falsely blaming the pestilence on poisoning by Jews." The pope also addressed the false claim that the Jews were responsible for initiating the plague: "It does not seem credible that the Jews on this occasion are responsible for the crime nor that they caused it, because this nearly universal pestilence . . . has afflicted and continues to afflict the Jews themselves" (Clement VI, *Sicut Judeis*, quoted in Aberth, *Black Death*, 159). The pope decreed the penalty of excommunication for anyone who harassed the Jews because of the pestilence.

The Pope Comes Home

In the year of the plague's arrival, twin girls were born on the Feast of the Annunciation to the wool dyer Jacopo Benincasa and his wife in Siena.

One twin, Giovanna, died in infancy; the other twin, Catherine, became one of the greatest female saints in Church history.

From an early age, Catherine followed a life of holiness and desired to become a Dominican tertiary, but her parents wanted marriage for their twenty-fifth child. Eventually her parents relented and allowed Catherine to enter a group of third-order Dominican laywomen known as the "Cloaked Sisters" in Siena. They wore a white woolen dress with a white veil and black cape, and lived in their own homes instead of in community. Catherine's rich spiritual life was nourished with locutions from Christ and visions of the Savior as well as numerous saints including the Blessed Mother, Sts. Peter and Paul, and St. Dominic. Catherine practiced extreme penances, such as eating only bread and vegetables, abstaining from wine, and sleeping only thirty minutes a night! Catherine's close relationship with Christ produced several unique spiritual blessings and gifts. She received the ability to know the state of souls. Those in a state of mortal sin reeked in her presence. In one instance, Catherine fled from the presence of a young and beautiful noblewoman, a cardinal's niece, because the woman had committed adultery and was a priest's mistress.[19] In 1370, Catherine received the gift of complete nourishment from the Eucharist; she required nothing else to eat to sustain her physical body. Near the end of her life, Catherine, like St. Francis before her, received the stigmata, but she requested the wounds remain invisible. While she suffered from the wounds of Christ physically, no one else could see them until they appeared outwardly upon her death.

Catherine's reputation for holiness spread throughout Christendom, and soon she was engaged in correspondence with people from every sector of medieval society, including popes and kings.[20] Catherine developed a unique relationship with the pope through her letters, calling him "our sweet Christ on earth" and "daddy." Her tone with the pope was, at times, very direct as she advised him on choosing virtuous cardinals, freeing the Church from overinvolvement in temporal politics, and returning his residence to Rome.

When her letters did not produce the return of the pope to Rome, Catherine traveled to Avignon to confront the pope and demand his return. She arrived in Avignon in June 1376 and remained through the summer. Years earlier Pope Gregory XI (r. 1370–1378) had made a private pledge to God while a cardinal that if he were ever elected pope, he would return the papal residence to Rome. Catherine received miraculous knowledge of this pledge and reminded Gregory of his promise when they met. Stunned, the pope agreed to return to Rome. Her mission complete, Catherine went back to Siena.

However, within a few months, Catherine received news that Gregory was wavering in his decision to leave France, so she wrote a stern letter to him:

> Do not delay, then, your coming. Do not believe the devil, who perceives his own loss, and so exerts himself to rob you of your possessions in order that you may lose your love and charity and your coming hindered. Respond to the Holy Spirit who calls you. I tell you, Come, come, come and do not wait for time, since time does not wait for you. I beg of you, on behalf of Christ crucified, that you be not a timorous child but manly. Open your mouth and swallow down the bitter for the sweet.[21]

The exhortation and persistence of St. Catherine finally bore fruit, and Pope Gregory XI entered Rome on January 17, 1377. The poor holy woman from Siena accomplished what seemed impossible through the sheer force of her will and the efficacy of her prayer.

Popes and Antipopes

The pope who returned to Rome died a little more than a year later. But before his death, in order to prevent a crisis, he stipulated that the conclave meet immediately after his passing and not wait for the long-distance cardinals to arrive. At the death of Gregory XI, there were sixteen cardinals in Rome (eleven French, four Italian, and one Spaniard) and seven cardinals not present (six in Avignon and one in Pisa). The assembled cardinals deliberated for ten days while the Roman people, fearing the election of a Frenchman would return the papacy to Avignon, demanded an Italian pope. The cardinals complied and chose Bartholomew Prignano, the archbishop of Bari, a dedicated reformist, who took the name Urban VI (r. 1378–1389).

The Roman people were happy, but the cardinals soon regretted their choice. Urban attempted to reform the Church by forcing changes on the cardinals and their way of life. He regulated their eating habits, denigrated them in public, and even physically assaulted one. His temper and abuse of the cardinals became well known, and fearing another crisis, St. Catherine wrote a letter telling him, "For the love of Jesus crucified, Holy Father, soften the sudden movements of your temper."[22] Unfortunately, the pope did not listen to the holy woman from Siena, and five months after the conclave, fifteen of the cardinals reassembled and declared their election of Urban VI null and void.

The cardinals justified their invalid action by declaring that their choice of Urban was coerced on account of the agitation of the Roman people. Then the rebellious cardinals, who had no authority to invalidate the previous papal election, elected Robert of Geneva as "pope." He took the name Clement VII. Hearing of their disobedient action and knowing the harm it would cause the Church, St. Catherine sent the three Italian cardinals who participated in the "anti-conclave" of 1378 a sternly worded letter:

> You clearly know the truth that Pope Urban VI is truly pope, chosen in orderly election, not influenced by fear. . . . What made you do this? The poison of self-love, which has infected the world. That is what makes you pillars lighter than straw— flowers which shed no perfume, but stench that makes the whole world reek! Now you want to corrupt this truth, and make us see the opposite, saying that you chose Pope Urban from fear, which is not so.[23]

Pope Urban VI excommunicated the antipope Clement VII and replaced the entire College of Cardinals. Antipope Clement VII attacked Rome but was defeated; he fled to Naples first and then to Avignon. The Great Western Schism, which afflicted Christendom for a generation, had begun.

Secular rulers backed either the validly elected pope or the antipope, and early in the fifteenth century there were three men simultaneously claiming to be pope. The scandal caused by the Great Western Schism further weakened the respect and authority of the pope among secular rulers and the lay faithful. Combined with pervasive ecclesiastical abuses and culminating with the Renaissance popes who followed, the crisis of the papacy in the fourteenth century laid the foundation for the revolt of Martin Luther and the beginnings of the Protestant movement, which would cleave the unity and faith that had been so vibrant in the Church in the Middle Ages.

Acknowledgments

I am deeply grateful to my wife, Kasey, and my children for their support and encouragement during this project.

Thanks are due to Jaymie Stuart Wolfe for approaching me to participate in this grand adventure of reclaiming Catholic history—may it bear much fruit in the life of the Church.

I also wish to thank King St. Louis IX for his saintly example, devotion to duty, love of Christ and the Church, and intercession during the writing of this manuscript.

Notes

Epigraph

1. Christopher Dawson, *The Formation of Christendom* (San Francisco: Ignatius Press, 2008 [1965]), 291.

Introduction: What's in a Name?

1. G. K. Chesterton, "The True Middle Ages," *Illustrated London News*, July 14, 1906.

2. Marcus Bull, *Thinking Medieval: An Introduction to the Study of the Middle Ages* (New York: Palgrave Macmillan, 2005), 47.

3. See Jamie Blosser, *Positively Medieval: The Surprising, Dynamic, Heroic Church of the Middle Ages* (Huntington, IN: Our Sunday Visitor, 2016), 15; and Bull, *Thinking Medieval*, 2.

4. See Bull, *Thinking Medieval*, 15.

1. Medieval Man in a Medieval World

1. Henri Daniel-Rops, *Cathedral and Crusade*, trans. John Warrington (New York: Dutton, 1963 [1957]), 2.

2. Dr. Carroll used this term as the title of the third volume in his History of Christendom series. He is also the founder of Christendom College in Front Royal, Virginia (https://www.christendom.edu).

3. See Daniel-Rops, *Cathedral and Crusade*, 28.

4. See Susan Reynolds, *Fiefs and Vassals: The Medieval Evidence Reinterpreted* (Oxford, UK: Clarendon Press, 1994), 476.

5. John of Salisbury, *Policraticus*. Quoted in *The Portable Medieval Reader*, ed. James Bruce Ross and Mary Martin McLaughlin (New York: Penguin, 1977 [1949]), 47.

6. Quoted in Reynolds, *Fiefs and Vassals*, 37.

7. The story is told in Daniel-Rops, *Cathedral and Crusade*, 32.

8. See Reynolds, *Fiefs and Vassals*. Reynolds argues the standard historical narrative is based on seventeenth- and eighteenth-century constructs. Medieval people did not use the terms *feudal, fiefs,* and *vassals*. Indeed, the term *vassal* is not found in German or French medieval documents.

9. Uta-Renate Blumenthal, *The Investiture Controversy: Church and Monarchy from the Ninth to the Twelfth Century* (Philadelphia: University of Pennsylvania Press, 1995 [1988]), 28.

10. Geoffrey Barraclough, *The Crucible of Europe: The Ninth and Tenth Centuries in European History* (Berkeley: University of California Press, 1976), 86.

11. See Marc Bloch, *Feudal Society*, vol. 2: *Social Classes and Political Organization*, trans. L. A. Manyon (Chicago: University of Chicago Press, 1961), 445.

12. Reynolds, *Fiefs and Vassals*, 33.

13. See Richard Abels, "The Historiography of a Construct: 'Feudalism' and the Medieval Historian," *History Compass* 7, no. 3 (2009): 1008–31.

14. Bloch, *Feudal Society*, 291.

15. See Frances Gies, *The Knight in History* (New York: Harper Perennial, 2011 [1987]), 3.

16. Daniel-Rops, *Cathedral and Crusade*, 280–81.

17. Jonathan Phillips, *The Fourth Crusade and the Sack of Constantinople* (New York: Viking Penguin, 2004), 40.

18. The decree from the Second Lateran Council stated, "We entirely forbid, moreover, these abominable jousts and tournaments in which knights come together by agreement and rashly engage in showing off their physical prowess and daring, and which often result in human deaths and danger to souls." *Decrees of the Ecumenical Councils*, ed. N. Tanner (Washington, DC, 1990), 1:199–200. Quoted in Phillips, *Fourth Crusade*, 44–45.

19. See Joseph Gies and Frances Gies, *Life in a Medieval Village* (New York: Harper Perennial, 2016 [1990]), 7.

20. See Joseph Gies and Frances Gies, *Life in a Medieval Castle* (New York: Harper Perennial, 2015 [1974]), 150.

21. The moldboard plow was made of iron instead of wood and was shaped like a knife. As the plow was pushed through the soil, the moldboard affixed behind the share turned over the earth, allowing for better nutrients to reach the planted crop. The horse was a faster and stronger animal than the ox, the regular plow animal. The three-field system of crop rotation divided a piece of land into three fields, two of which were used at one time for crops and the other left fallow for a season. The following season the fallow field was used for crops and another field was left fallow. This allowed for better utilization of land and increased the produce, which provided more food and led to an increase in population.

22. See Chris Wickham, *Medieval Europe* (New Haven, CT: Yale University Press, 2016), 121.

23. Ibid., 130.

24. Daniel-Rops, *Cathedral and Crusade*, 236.

25. Ibid., 58.

26. Daniel-Rops makes this point in *Cathedral and Crusade*, 368.

27. Daniel-Rops makes the argument that this style of architecture should be called the French style. See *Cathedral and Crusade*, 369.

28. Kenneth Clark, *Civilisation: A Personal View* (New York: Harper & Row, 1969), 56.

29. Daniel-Rops, *Cathedral and Crusade*, 252.

2. The Papal Reform Movement Begins

1. Quoted in Eamon Duffy, *Saints and Sinners: A History of the Popes* (New Haven, CT: Yale University Press, 2006), 128.

2. Blosser, *Positively Medieval*, 157–58.

3. The four popes of Cluny were St. Gregory VII (r. 1073–1085), Bl. Urban II (r. 1088–1099), Paschal II (r. 1099–1118), and Bl. Urban V (r. 1362–1370).

4. Warren H. Carroll, *The Building of Christendom*, vol. 2 of *A History of Christendom* (Front Royal, VA: Christendom College Press, 1987), 460.

5. Matthew Cullinan Hoffman, trans., *The Book of Gomorrah and St. Peter Damian's Struggle against Ecclesiastical Corruption* (New Braunfels, TX: Ite Ad Thomam Books and Media, 2015), 149.

6. Ibid., 82, 129.

7. Horace K. Mann, *The Lives of the Popes in the Middle Ages*, vol. 6 (London, 1910), 40. Quoted in Carroll, *Building of Christendom*, 466.

8. See Blumenthal, *Investiture Controversy*, 73.

9. The episode is recounted in Carroll, *Building of Christendom*, 472.

10. See Brian Tierney, *The Crisis of Church and State, 1050–1300* (Toronto: University of Toronto Press, 1988 [1964]), 27.

3. The Great Schism and Norman Conquest

1. Dawson, *Formation of Christendom*, 276.

2. Desiderius of Monte Cassino, 1.2. Quoted in Tom Holland, *The Forge of Christendom: The End of Days and the Epic Rise of the West* (New York: Doubleday, 2008), 272.

3. This point is made by Warren H. Carroll. See Carroll, *Building of Christendom*, 478.

4. E. Amann, "Michel Céulaire," in *Dictionnaire de Théologie catholique* X (2), 1683. Quoted in Carroll, *Building of Christendom*, 479.

5. Bernard Guillemain, *The Early Middle Ages* (New York: Hawthorn Books, 1960), 35.

6. Holland, *Forge of Christendom*, 279.

7. Quoted in Jean Comby, *How to Read Church History: From the Beginnings to the Fifteenth Century*, vol. 1 (New York: Crossroads, 2001), 132.

8. Quoted in Carroll, *Building of Christendom*, 481.

9. The twelve charges were as follows: (1) Cerularius had wrongly assumed the title of patriarch; (2) his supporters were guilty of simony; (3) eunuchs were ordained priests

and bishops, and some were purposefully castrated to ensure they became clerics; (4) rebaptism was required of Latin-rite Catholics living in the East; (5) priests were allowed to marry in the East; (6) the Ten Commandments were not obeyed; (7) the procession of the Holy Spirit from the Father and the Son was denied; (8) only leavened bread was valid matter for the Eucharist; (9) infants could not receive baptism until the eighth day after birth in accordance with Jewish purity laws; (10) clean-shaven men could not receive the Eucharist; (11) the Latin-rite celebration of the Mass was forbidden; and (12) papal authority had been defied in the East. The list is provided in Carroll, *Building of Christendom*, 496. The truthfulness of the charges is as follows: (1) false (only the use of the title "ecumenical patriarch" was forbidden); (2) true, for some supporters; (3) true; (4) false; (5) false (priests could be married before ordination, not afterward); (6) false; (7) true; (8) true, according to some Eastern theologians; (9) false; (10) false; (11) true; and (12) true.

10. Quoted in Comby, *How to Read Church History*, 133.

11. Quoted in Dawson, *Formation of Christendom*, 275.

12. Quoted in Henri Daniel-Rops, *The Protestant Reformation*, trans. Audrey Butler, vol. 1 (New York: Image, 1963), 131.

13. Pope St. Paul VI and Patriarch Athenagoras annulled the famous 1054 excommunications in 1965. Pope St. John Paul II and Pope Benedict XVI both worked tirelessly to bring about reunion. Sadly, the Eastern half of the Church is more fractured now than in the past and refuses to accept papal primacy and the overtures made to accommodate a mutual understanding of the main doctrines separating West and East.

14. David Howarth, *1066: The Year of Conquest* (New York: Penguin, 1977), 29.

15. Ibid., 12.

16. Ibid., 161.

17. *Hardrada* is thought to mean "hard bargainer" or "ruthless," "tough," and "stubborn." See Howarth, *1066*, 107.

18. Howarth describes the horrific scene: "One of them stabbed him in the chest, another cut off his head, another disemboweled him and the last cut off his leg at the thigh and carried it away." See Howarth, *1066*, 184.

19. Holland, *Forge of Christendom*, 328.

4. The Investiture Controversy

1. Quoted in Daniel-Rops, *Cathedral and Crusade*, 173.

2. There is some debate about Hildebrand's ecclesial status and training as a monk. Some historians distrust the traditional source that indicates Hildebrand was a monk.

3. Daniel-Rops, *Cathedral and Crusade*, 121.

4. Eamon Duffy, *Ten Popes Who Shook the World* (New Haven, CT: Yale University Press, 2011), Kindle, location 625.

5. Quoted in Guillemain, *Early Middle Ages*, 44.

6. The full list is found here: "Medieval Sourcebook: Gregory VII: *Dictatus Papae* 1090," Fordham University, last updated January 2, 2020, https://sourcebooks.fordham.edu.

7. Blumenthal, *Investiture Controversy*, 28.

8. Tierney, *Crisis of Church and State*, 51.

9. See Daniel-Rops, *Cathedral and Crusade*, 176.

10. King Henry IV, letter to Pope Gregory VII, in *Readings in Church History*, vol. 1: *From Pentecost to the Protestant Revolt*, ed. Colman J. Barry (Westminster, MD: Newman Press, 1960), 245.

11. Ibid.

12. *Register*, 3.10a. Quoted in Tierney, *Crisis of Church and State*, 61.

13. The Second Deposition of Henry (March 1080), trans. E. Emerton, in *Correspondence*, 149–52. Quoted in Tierney, *Crisis of Church and State*, 65.

14. Daniel-Rops, *Cathedral and Crusade*, 180.

15. For the Muslim troops in the Norman army, see Daniel-Rops, *Cathedral and Crusade*, 180; for the extent of the fire, see Tierney, *Crisis of Church and State*, 55.

16. Gregory VII, letter to all the faithful (1084), ed. E. Caspar, in *MGH Epistolae Selectae* II, 575. Quoted in Tierney, *Crisis of Church and State*, 73.

17. *Register*, appendix 3. Quoted in Tierney, *Crisis of Church and State*, 44.

18. See Daniel-Rops, *Cathedral and Crusade*, 182.

19. Blumenthal, *Investiture Controversy*, 173.

5. The Crusading Movement: Part 1

1. Jonathan Riley-Smith, *The Crusades, Christianity, and Islam* (New York: Columbia University Press, 2008), 40–41.

2. Holland, *Forge of Christendom*, 237.

3. Replicas of the church were built throughout France, and Jerusalem was a popular female name among the French nobility. See Riley-Smith, *First Crusaders*, 33.

4. Richard St. Vanne in 1026 and Ulrich of Breisgau in 1044 were stoned. Expulsion from the Sepulchre compound and closure of the pilgrim road occurred in 1055. A large group of German pilgrims led by Archbishop Siegfried of Mainz and Bishops Günther of Bamberg, Otto of Regensburg, and William of Utrecht were killed in 1065.

5. The Eastern Empire never called itself "Byzantine." The Protestant German scholar Hieronymus Wolf created that term in 1557. See Darío Fernández-Morera, *The Myth of the Andalusian Paradise* (Wilmington, DE: ISI Books, 2016), 75.

6. A detailed narrative of the crusades and a refutation of modern myths about the movement can be found in my book *The Glory of the Crusades* (El Cajon, CA: Catholic Answers Press, 2014).

7. This section is adapted from my article "The Council of Clermont: Beginning of the Crusades" for *Catholic Answers* online magazine, November 27, 2019, https://www.catholic.com.

8. Quoted in Daniel-Rops, *Cathedral and Crusade*, 133.

9. Robert the Monk, *Historia Hierosolymitana.* Quoted in *The First Crusade: The Chronicle of Fulcher of Chartres and Other Source Material*, ed. Edward Peters, 2nd ed. (Philadelphia: University of Pennsylvania Press, 1998), 28.

10. Ibid.

11. Robert the Monk's account has Urban saying, "They perforate their navels, and dragging forth the extremity of the intestines, bind it to a stake; then with flogging they lead the victim around until the viscera having gushed forth the victim falls prostrate upon the ground. Others they bind to a post and pierce with arrows. Others they compel to extend their necks and then, attacking them with naked swords attempt to cut through the neck with a single blow." See Robert the Monk, *Historia Hierosolymitana*, in Peters, *First Crusade*, 27.

12. Ibid.

13. Canon of the Council of Clermont in Peters, *First Crusade*, 37.

14. Ane L. Bysted, *The Crusade Indulgence: Spiritual Rewards and the Theology of the Crusades, Ca. 1095–1216*, in *History of Warfare*, vol. 103 (Boston: Brill, 2015), 5.

15. John France, "Patronage and the Appeal of the First Crusade," in *The Crusades: The Essential Readings*, ed. Thomas F. Madden (Malden, MA: Blackwell, 2006), 195–96. France also illustrates the extent of Urban's preaching and the significant response it engendered by comparing the populations of France, Italy, Germany, and England in the late eleventh century, which was estimated at twenty million people, with the populations of those same countries in the modern world, which is 264 million people. Applying the same ratio of population to crusade respondents produces a modern number of crusaders at 1.3 million people!

16. Jonathan Riley-Smith, *The Crusades: A History*, 2nd ed. (New Haven, CT: Yale University Press, 2005), 20.

17. "Bohemond" was a nickname given by his father, Robert Guiscard. The reference was to a legendary giant since the infant was big and strong; his baptismal name was Mark. See Christopher Tyerman, *God's War: A New History of the Crusades* (Cambridge, MA: Belknap Press of Harvard University Press, 2006), 114.

18. Daniel-Rops, *Cathedral and Crusade*, 440.

19. Fulcher of Chartres, *Chronicle*, Book I, XVI.2. Quoted in Peters, *First Crusade*, 73.

20. The number marching to Jerusalem is taken from the chronicler Raymond d'Aguilers and quoted in John France, *Victory in the East: A Military History of the First Crusade* (New York: Cambridge University Press, 1994), 3.

21. A more detailed examination of this historical episode can be found in my book *The Glory of the Crusades*, 74–77.

22. The chronicles record "blood up to the ankles" or "up to the knees of horses." These images were meant to recall Revelation 14:20 and expressed the victory of God's people over their opponent and his judgment on infidels. For more information on this topic, see Benjamin Z. Kedar, "The Jerusalem Massacre of 1099 in the Western Historiography of the Crusades," in *Crusades*, vol. 3, Society for the Study of the Crusades and the Latin East (Burlington, VT: Ashgate, 2004).

23. See Riley-Smith, *First Crusaders*, 161.

24. Amin Maalouf, *The Crusades through Arab Eyes*, trans. Jon Rothschild (New York: Schocken Books, 1984), 135.

25. Theophilus Reynauld wrote *The Gallic Bee* in the sixteenth century and referred to St. Bernard as the "Mellifluous" or "Honey-Sweet" Doctor of the Church, a name that has stuck down through the centuries. Pope Pius XII used this description in the title for his encyclical on St. Bernard in 1953 on the eight hundredth anniversary of his death. Bernard, "a diligent bee, has extracted the sweet essence from Scripture and the Fathers and refined it in loving meditation." See Christopher Rengers, *The 33 Doctors of the Church* (Rockford, IL: Tan Books, 2000), 282.

26. Hannes Möhring, *Saladin: The Sultan and His Times, 1138–1193*, trans. David S. Bachrach, introduction and preface by Paul M. Cobb (Baltimore: Johns Hopkins University Press, 2005), xviii.

27. Estimate of strength is taken from France, *Victory in the East*, 136. For the army taking three days to pass a single point, see Tyerman, *God's War*, 418.

28. There is some debate in academic circles over whether Isaac actually entered into the treaty. Both Riley-Smith (*The Crusades*, 139) and Thomas F. Madden (*The New Concise History of the Crusades*, updated ed. [New York: Rowman & Littlefield, 2005], 80) agree he did, but Savva Neocleous in "The Byzantines and Saladin: Opponents of the Third Crusade?" in *Crusades*, vol. 9, Society for the Study of the Crusades and the Latin East (Burlington, VT: Ashgate, 2010), 87–106, argues differently.

29. Riley-Smith, *The Crusades*, 141.

30. Richard met his end due to the most perplexing case of literally lowering one's guard. Inspecting the siege progress at twilight, the king noticed on the ramparts a lone figure of a common soldier with a crossbow whose only protection was a frying pan. Awed by the man's audacity and courage, Richard lowered his shield and clapped in applause. Richard's display of chivalrous acknowledgment did not impress the soldier, who dropped his frying pan and let loose his bolt. The "extraordinarily well-aimed shot" hit Richard in the left shoulder. An unskilled surgeon attempted to remove the arrowhead, but the tissue damage from the surgery was extensive. Gangrene set in to the wound, and two weeks later the great crusader at the age of forty-two was dead. See Warren H. Carroll, *The Glory of Christendom*, vol. 3 of *A History of Christendom* (Front Royal, VA: Christendom College Press, 1993), 148.

6. The Crusading Movement: Part 2

1. Quoted in Tyerman, *God's War*, 477–78.

2. One biographer noted, "Innocent, like other great historical figures, has suffered from being judged in the light of later events and on different terms from his own." Jane Sayers, *Innocent III: Leader of Europe, 1198–1216* (New York: Longman, 1994), 193.

3. See Daniel-Rops, *Cathedral and Crusade*, 138.

4. See Tierney, *Crisis of Church and State*, 130.

5. Byzantine emperors used the term to highlight their role in Church affairs. St. Bernard of Clairvaux used it in reference to the popes, and Adrian IV (r. 1154–1159) was the first pope to use the title.

6. *Sermo* II, PL 217, col. 656. Quoted in Sayers, *Innocent III*, 91.

7. Letter to the prefect Acerbus and the nobles of Tuscany (1198), PL 214, col. 377. Quoted in Sayers, *Innocent III*, 197.

8. Tyerman, *God's War*, 480.

9. Riley-Smith, *The Crusades*, 148–49.

10. A modern comparison of the immense request of the crusaders is a "major international airline ceasing flights for a year to prepare its planes for one particular client, and then to serve that client exclusively for a further period afterwards." See Phillips, *Fourth Crusade*, 61.

11. Vitaliano Brunelli, *Storia della città di Zara* (Venice: Istituto Veneto di Arti Grafiche, 1913), 361. Quoted in Donald E. Queller and Thomas F. Madden, *The Fourth Crusade: The Conquest of Constantinople*, 2nd ed. (Philadelphia: University of Pennsylvania Press, 1997), 56.

12. *Devastatio Constantinopolitana*, in *Contemporary Sources for the Fourth Crusade*, by A. J. Andrea (Leiden, Netherlands: Brill, 2000), 216. Quoted in Tyerman, *God's War*, 541.

13. Villehardouin, *Conquête de Constantinople*, sec. 165, I:166. Quoted in Queller and Madden, *Fourth Crusade*, 122.

14. Mann, *Lives of the Popes*, 12:266–67; Mary Purcell, *St. Anthony and His Times* (Dublin: M. H. Gill and Son, 1960), 26. Quoted in Carroll, *Glory of Christendom*, 158.

15. The point is made by Phillips. See Phillips, *Fourth Crusade*, 311.

16. For the number of participants, see Sophia Menache, *The Vox Dei: Communication in the Middle Ages* (New York: Oxford University Press, 1990), 56. Cited in Sayers, *Innocent III*, 130, and Daniel-Rops, *Cathedral and Crusade*, 229. For the presence of Francis and Dominic, see Carroll, *Glory of Christendom*, 187.

17. Oliver of Paderborn, *The Capture of Damietta*. Quoted in Madden, *New Concise History of the Crusades*, 151.

18. Salimbene, *The Emperor Frederick II*. Quoted in Ross and McLaughlin, *Portable Medieval Reader*, 365.

19. When Constance of Aragon, Frederick's first wife, died in 1222, he married Isabella II, the daughter of John of Brienne (of Fifth Crusade fame), who was regent for the Kingdom of Jerusalem. John feared that Frederick desired the throne for himself and stipulated the emperor could not marry his daughter unless he promised not to claim the throne of Jerusalem until after John's death. Frederick agreed, but after the wedding reneged on his promise and removed John as regent. Sadly, Isabella II died in childbirth at the age of sixteen. The child, Conrad, was the rightful heir to the throne but as an infant could not assume the responsibilities.

20. *Gestes des Chyprois.* Quoted in Régine Pernoud, *The Crusaders*, trans. Enid Grant (San Francisco: Ignatius Press, 2003), 291.

21. Mann, *Lives of the Popes*, 15:72–75. Quoted in Carroll, *Glory of Christendom*, 242.

22. The term is Régine Pernoud's. See *The Crusaders*, 274.

23. Joinville quoted in Ross and McLaughlin, *Portable Medieval Reader*, 375.

24. See Daniel-Rops, *Cathedral and Crusade*, 294.

25. Jacques Le Goff, *Saint Louis*, trans. Gareth Evan Gollrad (Notre Dame: University of Notre Dame Press, 2009), 204.

26. Ibid., 630.

27. Ibid., 625.

28. See William of Saint-Pathus, *Vie de Saint Louis*, ed. Henri-François Delaborde (Paris, 1899), 39. Quoted in Le Goff, *Saint Louis*, 624.

29. William of Saint-Pathus, *Vie de Saint Louis*, 123. Quoted in Le Goff, *Saint Louis*, 622.

30. *Saint Louis' Advice to His Son.* Quoted in *Medieval Civilization*, trans. and ed. Dana Munro and George Clarke Sellery (New York: Century, 1910), 366–75.

31. For the time of Louis's death, see *Vita*, in *Recueil des historiens des Gaules et de la France*, 20:23. Quoted in Le Goff, *Saint Louis*, 226. For his final words, see Carroll, *Glory of Christendom*, 294.

7. Crisis in England and the Beggar Monks

1. Carroll, *Glory of Christendom*, 161.

2. The 1964 movie *Becket*, with Richard Burton as Thomas Becket, erroneously depicts him as a Saxon.

3. Giraldus Cambrensis, *Henry II, King of England.* Quoted in Ross and McLaughlin, *Portable Medieval Reader*, 357–58.

4. Richard Winston, *Thomas Becket* (London: Constable, 1967), 153. Quoted in Carroll, *Glory of Christendom*, 77.

5. Carroll, *Glory of Christendom*, 106.

6. Taken from Roger of Hoveden's account, in Blosser, *Positively Medieval*, 129.

7. Ibid., 130.

8. Ibid.

9. Carroll, *Glory of Christendom*, 106. St. Alphege was the archbishop of Canterbury martyred by the Danes in 1012.

10. Ibid.

11. Desmond Seward, *Eleanor of Aquitaine: The Mother Queen of the Middle Ages* (New York: Pegasus Books, 2014 [1978]), 120.

12. See Dawson, *Formation of Christendom*, 225.

13. Thomas of Celano, in Blosser, *Positively Medieval*, 170.

14. Ibid., 171.

15. Carroll, *Glory of Christendom*, 162.

16. Daniel-Rops, *Cathedral and Crusade*, 159.

17. Frank M. Rega, *St. Francis of Assisi and the Conversion of the Muslims* (Rockford, IL: TAN Books, 2007), 23.

18. Jordan of Giano, *How the Friars Came to Germany*. Quoted in Ross and McLaughlin, *Portable Medieval Reader*, 59.

19. Rega, *St. Francis of Assisi*, 102.

20. Thomas of Celano, in Blosser, *Positively Medieval*, 174.

21. Daniel-Rops, *Cathedral and Crusade*, 158.

22. Blosser, *Positively Medieval*, 161.

23. Daniel-Rops, *Cathedral and Crusade*, 149.

24. Ibid., 161.

8. Medieval Inquisitors and Scholars

1. Daniel-Rops, *Cathedral and Crusade*, 520.

2. Joseph R. Strayer, *The Albigensian Crusades* (Ann Arbor: University of Michigan Press, 1992 [1971]), 19.

3. See Carroll, *Glory of Christendom*, 165.

4. Riley-Smith, *The Crusades*, 165.

5. See Daniel-Rops, *Cathedral and Crusade*, 532.

6. Daniel-Rops, *Cathedral and Crusade*, 538.

7. Guillemain, *Early Middle Ages*, 115.

8. See Sayers, *Innocent III*, 106.

9. St. Raymond's book was the last major change to canon law until the 1917 Code of St. Pius X, which was revised by St. John Paul II in the 1983 code.

10. Edward Peters, *Torture*, expanded ed. (Philadelphia: University of Pennsylvania Press, 1985), 41.

11. Joseph Gies and Frances Gies, *Life in a Medieval City* (New York: Harper Perennial, 1981 [2016]), 205.

12. Peters, *Torture*, 46.

13. William Thomas Walsh, *Characters of the Inquisition* (Rockford, IL: TAN Books, 1987 [1940]), 86.

14. Daniel-Rops, *Cathedral and Crusade*, 306.

15. Rodney Stark, *Bearing False Witness: Debunking Centuries of Anti-Catholic History* (West Conshohocken, PA: Templeton Press, 2016), 140.

16. Ibid., 85.

17. Quoted in Thomas E. Woods Jr., *How the Catholic Church Built Western Civilization* (Washington, DC: Regnery, 2005), 65.

18. Daniel-Rops, *Cathedral and Crusade*, 312.

19. Ibid., 322.

20. Bruno Scott James, *St. Bernard of Clairvaux* (New York: Harper and Brothers, 1957), 139–40. Quoted in Carroll, *Glory of Christendom*, 52.

21. Guillemain, *Early Middle Ages*, 86.

22. Benedict XVI, Wednesday General Audience on Saint Thomas Aquinas, June 2, 2010, in *Holy Men and Women of the Middle Ages and Beyond* (San Francisco: Ignatius Press, 2012), 7.

9. Trouble in the Papacy

1. Catherine of Siena, "Letter to Pope Gregory XI," in *Saint Catherine of Siena as Seen in Her Letters*, ed. Vida D. Scudder (New York: Dutton, 1906), 131.

2. Daniel-Rops, *Cathedral and Crusade*, 224.

3. This insight is from Jon M. Sweeney, *The Pope Who Quit: A True Medieval Tale of Mystery, Death, and Salvation* (New York: Image Books, 2012), 22–23.

4. Odoricus Rainaldi, *Annales Ecclesiastici*, 20. Quoted in Sweeney, *Pope Who Quit*, 195–96.

5. See Tierney, *Crisis of Church and State*, 173.

6. Georges Digard, *Philippe le Bel et le Saint-Siège de 1285 à 1304* (Paris: Sirey, 1936), 2:29; Franklin J. Pegues, *The Lawyers of the Last Capetians* (Princeton, NJ: Princeton University Press, 1962), 99. Quoted in Carroll, *Glory of Christendom*, 334.

7. See Tierney, *Crisis of Church and State*, 173.

8. Boniface VIII, *Ausculta fili*. Quoted in Tierney, *Crisis of Church and State*, 186.

9. Daniel-Rops, *Cathedral and Crusade*, 573.

10. See Tierney, *Crisis of Church and State*, 189.

11. Daniel-Rops, *Cathedral and Crusade*, 574.

12. The term *black death* is a modern one. It was first coined in the sixteenth century and popularized in the nineteenth century. Contemporaries called the infection "the pestilence," "the plague," and the "great mortality." See John Aberth, *The Black Death: The Great Mortality of 1348–1350; A Brief History with Documents* (New York: Bedford/St. Martin's, 2005), 1; and Norman Cantor, *In the Wake of the Plague: The Black Death and the World It Made* (New York: Harper, 2001), 7.

13. Poland and Bohemia were noted exceptions. See Aberth, *Black Death*, 2.

14. Ibid., vii and 3.

15. Michele da Piazza, *Chronicle*. Quoted in Aberth, *Black Death*, 29.

16. Jacme d'Agramont, *Regimen of Protection against Epidemics*. Quoted in Aberth, *Black Death*, 54. The plague affected daily hygiene as people changed washing and bathing habits, which had been frequent in the medieval period before the plague. See Cantor, *In the Wake of the Plague*, 22–23.

17. Ibid., 69.

18. See Brennan Pursell, *History in His Hands: A Christian Narrative of the West* (New York: Crossroad, 2011), 151; and Cantor, *In the Wake of the Plague*, 206.

19. See Sigrid Undset, *Catherine of Siena*, trans. Kate Austin-Lund (San Francisco: Ignatius Press, 2009 [1954]), 77.

20. For most of her life Catherine dictated letters to those who could write since she could not, but a few years before her death, Catherine received the gift of writing in a miraculous manner. She is considered the greatest Italian letter writer of the fourteenth century after Petrarch.

21. Catherine of Siena, "Letter to Pope Gregory XI," in *Saint Catherine of Siena as Seen in Her Letters*, ed. Vida D. Scudder (New York: Dutton, 1906), 132, 185.

22. Philip Hughes, *A Popular History of the Catholic Church* (New York: Image, 1947), 144.

23. *Saint Catherine of Siena as Seen in Her Letters*, 278.

For Further Reading

Aberth, John. *The Black Death: The Great Mortality of 1348–1350; A Brief History with Documents*. New York: Bedford/St. Martin's, 2005.

Blosser, Jamie. *Positively Medieval: The Surprising, Dynamic, Heroic Church of the Middle Ages*. Huntington, IN: Our Sunday Visitor, 2016.

Blumenthal, Uta-Renate. *The Investiture Controversy: Church and Monarchy from the Ninth to the Twelfth Century*. Philadelphia: University of Pennsylvania Press, 1995 [1988].

Bull, Marcus. *Thinking Medieval: An Introduction to the Study of the Middle Ages*. New York: Palgrave Macmillan, 2005.

Carroll, Warren H. *The Building of Christendom*. Vol. 2 of *A History of Christendom*. Front Royal, VA: Christendom College Press, 1987.

———. *The Glory of Christendom*. Vol. 3 of *A History of Christendom*. Front Royal, VA: Christendom College Press, 1993.

Catherine of Siena. *Saint Catherine of Siena as Seen in Her Letters*, edited by Vida D. Scudder. New York: Dutton, 1906.

Daniel-Rops, Henri. *Cathedral and Crusade*. Translated by John Warrington. New York: Dutton, 1963 [1957].

Duffy, Eamon. *Saints and Sinners: A History of the Popes*. New Haven, CT: Yale University Press, 2006.

Gies, Joseph, and Frances Gies. *Life in a Medieval Village*. New York: Harper Perennial, 2016 [1990].

———. *Life in a Medieval Castle*. New York: Harper Perennial, 2015 [1974].

Hoffman, Matthew Cullinan, trans. *The Book of Gomorrah and St. Peter Damian's Struggle against Ecclesiastical Corruption*. New Braunfels, TX: Ite Ad Thomam Books and Media, 2015.

Kamen, Henry. *The Spanish Inquisition: A Historical Revision*. New Haven, CT: Yale University Press, 1997.

Le Goff, Jacques. *Saint Louis*. Translated by Gareth Evan Gollrad. Notre Dame: University of Notre Dame Press, 2009.

Madden, Thomas F. *The New Concise History of the Crusades*. Updated ed. New York: Rowman & Littlefield, 2005.

Pernoud, Régine. *The Crusaders*. Translated by Enid Grant. San Francisco: Ignatius Press, 2003.

———. *Those Terrible Middle Ages: Debunking the Myths*. Translated by Anne Englund Nash. San Francisco: Ignatius Press, 2000 [1977].

Peters, Edward. *Inquisition*. Berkeley: University of California Press, 1988.

———. *Torture*. Expanded ed. Philadelphia: University of Pennsylvania Press, 1985.

Queller, Donald E., and Thomas F. Madden. *The Fourth Crusade: The Conquest of Constantinople*. 2nd ed. Philadelphia: University of Pennsylvania Press, 1997.

Rega, Frank M. *St. Francis of Assisi and the Conversion of the Muslims*. Rockford, IL: TAN Books, 2007.

Riley-Smith, Jonathan. *The First Crusaders, 1095–1131*. Cambridge: Cambridge University Press, 1997.

Strayer, Joseph R. *The Albigensian Crusades*. Ann Arbor: University of Michigan Press, 1992 [1971].

Tierney, Brian. *The Crisis of Church and State, 1050–1300*. Toronto: University of Toronto Press, 1988 [1964].

Tyerman, Christopher. *God's War: A New History of the Crusades*. Cambridge, MA: Belknap Press of Harvard University Press, 2006.

Weidenkopf, Steve. *The Glory of the Crusades*. El Cajon, CA: Catholic Answers Press, 2014.

———. *The Real Story of Catholic History: Answering Twenty Centuries of Anti-Catholic Myths*. El Cajon, CA: Catholic Answers Press, 2017.

———. *Timeless: A History of the Catholic Church*. Huntington, IN: Our Sunday Visitor Press, 2019.

Index